Perfect Days of Fun Things to Do in Retirement

Big Ideas for What to Do in Retirement

Moe Barnes

Copyright © 2023
All rights reserved.

The content contained within this book may not be reproduced, duplicated or transmitted without direct written permission from the author or the publisher. Under no circumstances will any blame or legal responsibility be held against the publisher, or author, for any damages, reparation, or monetary loss due to the information contained within this book. Either directly or indirectly.

Legal Notice:
This book is copyright protected. This book is only for personal use. You cannot amend, distribute, sell, use, quote or paraphrase any part, or the content within this book, without the consent of the author or publisher.

Disclaimer Notice:
Please note the information contained within this document is for educational and entertainment purposes only. All effort has been executed to present accurate, up to date, and reliable, complete information. No warranties of any kind are declared or implied. Readers acknowledge that the author is not engaging in the rendering of legal, financial, medical or professional advice. The content within this book has been derived from various sources. Please consult a licensed professional before attempting any techniques outlined in this book.

By reading this document, the reader agrees that under no circumstances is the author responsible for any losses, direct or indirect, which are incurred as a result of the use of information contained within this document, including, but not limited to, errors, omissions, or inaccuracies.

TABLE OF CONTENTS

Introduction — 6
Why Retirement is the Perfect Time for Fun
Embracing the Irreverent, Outrageous, and Funny

Getting Active in Nature — 10
Local Parks and Hiking Trails
Birdwatching and Wildlife Spotting
Gardening for Fun and Health
Fishing and Boating Excursions
Geocaching and Treasure Hunting
Walking or hiking groups
Beekeeping
Mushroom cultivation

Travel and Adventure — 32
Road Trips Across the Country
Discovering Hidden Gems in Your Own City
Cruising the High Seas
Exploring National Parks and UNESCO Sites
Embarking on Solo or Group Travel Adventures
Volunteering Abroad: Combining Travel and Service
Participating in Educational and Cultural Tours
Exploring the World through Home Exchanges
Travel and Exploration

Creative Pursuits — 53
Painting and Drawing for Beginners
Crafting Your Way to Happiness
Writing and Journaling for Personal Growth
Pottery and Ceramics
Performing Arts: Acting, Singing, and Dancing
Homebrewing

Hobbies and Interests — 65
Picking Up a New Instrument
Painting, Drawing, and Sculpting
Photography: Capturing Life's Beauty
Joining a Book Club

Sports and Fitness   70
  Swimming for Health and Relaxation
  Golfing: A Social and Competitive Sport
  Yoga and Meditation for Mind and Body Wellness
  Cycling Adventures
  Low-Impact Sports and Games
  Tai Chi and Qigong for Balance and Flexibility
  Exploring Alternative Therapies and Treatments
  Water Aerobics and Aquatic Exercises

Technology and Entertainment   80
  Embracing New Technologies and Gadgets
  Exploring Virtual Reality and Video Games
  Creating a Home Theater Experience
  Discovering New Music, Podcasts, and Audiobooks

Fun with Family and Friends   90
  Organizing Family Reunions and Get-Togethers
  Board Game and Puzzle Nights
  Movie and TV Show Marathons
  Hosting Theme Parties and Potlucks
  Attending Local Festivals and Events
  Game Nights with Friends and Family
  Movie and Theatre Outings
  Potlucks, Picnics, and Social Gatherings

Educational Pursuits   107
  Online Courses and Webinars
  Museum and Art Gallery Visits
  Attending Local Science and Technology Fairs
  Learning a New Language
  Exploring Your Genealogy and Family History
  Attending Lectures and Workshops

Conclusion   122
  Creating a Fulfilling and Purposeful Retirement
  Embracing Change and New Opportunities

INTRODUCTION: THE JOYFUL JOURNEY OF RETIREMENT

Retirement is often seen as the golden years, a time to relax and enjoy the fruits of one's labour after a lifetime of hard work. It is a period of life that brings with it a wealth of opportunities and the chance to embark on a joyful journey full of laughter, adventure and personal growth. With this in mind, Fun Things to Do in Retirement has been created to inspire and guide retirees through an exciting exploration of life's possibilities.

In this book, we begin by exploring the importance of embracing a light-hearted approach to life at this stage. After decades of dedication to career and family, retirement offers a unique opportunity for individuals to rediscover their passions, pursue new interests and find joy in the simple pleasures of life. The key to a fulfilling retirement is to maintain a sense of wonder and curiosity, and an openness to trying new things.

As we age, it is important to recognise the role of laughter and play in our lives. Laughter has many health benefits, such as reducing stress, boosting the immune system and promoting a sense of well-being. Play, on the other hand, keeps us mentally agile and fosters creativity, allowing us to explore our world with a renewed sense of excitement. By incorporating humour and playfulness into our daily lives, we can enhance our retirement experience and cultivate a youthful spirit.

This book also emphasises the importance of making meaningful connections and fostering a sense of community. As social beings, we thrive on companionship, shared experiences and mutual support. By seeking out like-minded individuals, joining clubs or social groups, and engaging in activities that bring us joy, we can create a vibrant and fulfilling social life in retirement.

This introduction explores the idea of giving back and making a difference in the world during our retirement years. By volunteering our time, sharing our wisdom or performing acts of kindness, we can contribute to the well-being of others and experience a sense of purpose and satisfaction.

Finally, the Joyful Journey of Retirement encourages retirees to embrace the benefits of technology to enhance their retirement experience. From staying connected with friends and family to exploring new worlds through virtual reality, technology can open doors to endless entertainment and social opportunities.

The Joyful Journey of Retirement invites retirees to take a light-hearted, adventurous and fulfilling approach to life after work. By focusing on laughter, play, social connection, personal growth and giving back, retirees can create a rich and rewarding retirement experience that brings joy, meaning and purpose to their golden years.

Why Retirement is the Perfect Time for Fun

Retirement is often regarded as the culmination of one's professional life, a time to reap the rewards of hard work and dedication. It is a period of transition, where individuals shift from the daily grind of work to a life filled with newfound freedom and opportunity. This makes retirement the perfect time for fun, as it offers the chance to explore, experiment, and embrace the joys that life has to offer.

One of the main reasons retirement is the ideal time for fun is the abundance of leisure time available. With the absence of work-related responsibilities, retirees have the freedom to pursue their interests and engage in activities that bring them happiness. This newfound time can be spent on hobbies, travel, socializing, or even learning new skills. The possibilities are virtually limitless, allowing retirees to create a fulfilling and enjoyable lifestyle tailored to their preferences.

Another reason retirement is a prime time for fun is the opportunity for personal growth and self-discovery. Throughout our working years, many of us become defined by our careers, often neglecting other aspects of our lives. Retirement offers a chance to redefine ourselves, to explore our passions, and to rediscover aspects of our personalities that may have been dormant for years. This process of self-discovery can be exciting, empowering, and incredibly rewarding, as we learn to embrace our authentic selves and find joy in the many facets of our lives.

Additionally, retirement allows us to prioritize our well-being and focus on activities that promote physical, mental, and emotional health. Engaging in fun and enjoyable pursuits can have a profound impact on our overall health, as it helps to reduce stress, increase mental agility, and foster a sense of happiness and satisfaction. The act of having fun can be both therapeutic and rejuvenating, providing retirees with the opportunity to prioritize their well-being and invest in their quality of life.

The social aspect of retirement is another significant factor that makes it the perfect time for fun. As we age, maintaining meaningful relationships and staying connected to others becomes increasingly important for our overall well-being. Retirement offers the chance to strengthen existing bonds, forge new friendships, and build a supportive community of like-minded individuals who share our interests and zest for life. By engaging in fun activities together, we can create lasting memories, deepen our connections, and enrich our retirement experience.

Retirement provides the opportunity to leave a lasting legacy and make a difference in the world. By dedicating time and energy to causes we are passionate about, volunteering, or mentoring others, we can create a positive impact on our communities and beyond. The pursuit of fun in retirement can be a powerful force for change, as it inspires others to live life to the fullest and embrace the endless possibilities that life has to offer.

Retirement is the perfect time for fun, as it presents a unique opportunity to explore, grow, and find joy in the many experiences life has to offer. By embracing the freedom, time, and opportunities that retirement provides, we can create a fulfilling and enjoyable life after work, filled with laughter, adventure, and personal growth.

Embracing the Irreverent, Outrageous, and Funny

In a world that often seems to take itself too seriously, embracing the irreverent, outrageous, and funny can be a breath of fresh air, especially during retirement. As we step away from our careers and into this new phase of life, it's important to remember that fun, laughter, and a sense of play are essential ingredients for a fulfilling and enjoyable retirement experience. By embracing the unconventional, we can challenge age stereotypes, forge strong connections, and discover a newfound zest for life.

Irreverence means not being afraid to push boundaries and question the status quo. In retirement, this can translate to exploring unconventional hobbies, participating in surprising activities, or simply adopting a lighthearted attitude towards life. Embracing the irreverent encourages us to break free from the constraints of societal expectations and forge our own unique path. This can be incredibly empowering, as it allows us to live authentically and discover new passions and interests that may have been neglected during our working years.

Outrageousness, on the other hand, is all about daring to be bold, taking risks, and indulging in experiences that may seem unconventional or even eccentric. In retirement, this can involve engaging in extreme sports, embarking on unusual travel adventures, or joining social clubs that celebrate the peculiar and offbeat. By embracing the outrageous, we can challenge age stereotypes and demonstrate that retirement is not about fading into the background but rather about living life to the fullest, with gusto and enthusiasm.

The funny side of life is equally important in retirement, as laughter has numerous benefits for our physical, mental, and emotional well-being. By seeking out humor in everyday situations, enjoying comedic movies, books, or performances, and even participating in laughter yoga or other laughter-based activities, we can cultivate a sense of joy and lightness that enriches our lives. Laughter has the power to strengthen social bonds, reduce stress, and promote a sense of happiness and contentment, making it an invaluable ingredient for a fulfilling retirement.

Moreover, embracing the irreverent, outrageous, and funny can have a positive impact on our relationships and social lives. By seeking out like-minded individuals who share our appreciation for the unconventional, we can build a supportive community of friends who encourage and inspire us to continue exploring life's possibilities. These connections can be instrumental in helping us maintain a sense of purpose and belonging as we navigate the challenges and joys of retirement.

Embracing the irreverent, outrageous, and funny during retirement can lead to a richer, more rewarding, and enjoyable life experience. By challenging societal expectations, pursuing unconventional interests, and cultivating a sense of humor, we can create a retirement that is both meaningful and fun. The benefits of this approach are numerous, from personal growth and self-discovery to improved well-being and strengthened social connections. So, as you embark on your retirement journey, don't be afraid to embrace the unconventional and let laughter, adventure, and playfulness guide you towards a life filled with joy and fulfillment.

GETTING ACTIVE IN NATURE WHEN RETIREMENT

Embrace the beauty of nature and enjoy your retirement by participating in various outdoor activities. This section will provide an overview of diverse ways to stay active and engaged with the environment while ensuring a fulfilling retired life.

Retirement presents an excellent opportunity to reconnect with nature and engage in various outdoor activities that not only keep you physically active but also contribute to your mental well-being. This stage in life allows you to take control of your schedule, providing ample time to explore the great outdoors and enjoy nature's tranquility.

Physical Benefits of Getting Active in Nature

Staying active in nature provides numerous physical benefits. Outdoor activities, such as walking, hiking, and gardening, promote cardiovascular health, increase muscle strength, and improve flexibility. Engaging in regular exercise can also help you maintain a healthy weight, reduce the risk of chronic diseases, and increase your overall energy levels.

Moreover, exposure to sunlight enables your body to produce vitamin D, which is crucial for maintaining strong bones and supporting your immune system. Spending time in natural settings can also improve your sleep quality, as exposure to natural light helps regulate your circadian rhythm.

Mental Health Benefits of Getting Active in Nature

Nature has a powerful impact on mental health. Engaging in outdoor activities can help reduce stress, anxiety, and depression by encouraging relaxation and providing a sense of calm. The natural environment stimulates the release of endorphins, which can improve your mood and promote feelings of happiness.

Being active in nature also encourages mindfulness, allowing you to focus on the present moment and appreciate the beauty of your surroundings. This mindfulness practice can enhance your cognitive abilities, including memory, attention, and problem-solving skills.

Social Benefits of Getting Active in Nature

Participating in outdoor activities with others can strengthen social bonds and improve your sense of community. Joining local groups or clubs dedicated to nature-related pursuits allows you to connect with like-minded individuals who share your interests. By engaging in group activities, you can build new friendships, expand your social network, and combat feelings of isolation and loneliness.

Exploring New Hobbies and Interests

Getting active in nature during retirement presents an opportunity to explore new hobbies and interests. From birdwatching to geocaching, there is a wide range of activities to suit different preferences and abilities. Trying new activities can stimulate your curiosity, boost your self-confidence, and provide a sense of accomplishment.

Retirement is the perfect time to get active in nature and reap the physical, mental, and social benefits it offers. By exploring new outdoor activities and connecting with fellow nature enthusiasts, you can create a fulfilling and healthy retirement experience that enriches your life and overall well-being.

Local Parks and WALKING Trails

Local parks and hiking trails offer a wealth of opportunities for retirees to stay active, connect with nature, and explore their surroundings. Taking advantage of these natural settings can lead to a multitude of physical, mental, and social benefits, making them an essential part of a fulfilling retirement.

Visiting local parks provides retirees with easy access to green spaces and recreational facilities, promoting physical activity and overall well-being. Parks often feature walking paths, playgrounds, and sports courts that can be utilized for various low-impact exercises. These activities can help improve cardiovascular health, maintain a healthy weight, and enhance flexibility.

Walking trails, on the other hand, offer a more challenging form of physical activity, encouraging retirees to build endurance, stamina and strength. Walking can also improve balance and coordination, which are important factors in maintaining independence and preventing falls as we age.

In addition to the physical benefits, spending time in parks and on trails can significantly improve mental health. The natural environment promotes relaxation, helping to reduce stress, anxiety and depression. Exposure to nature can also have a positive impact on cognitive abilities, including memory, attention and problem-solving skills. The sights, sounds and smells of nature can provide sensory stimulation that promotes mindfulness and a deeper connection to the natural world.

Local parks and trails also serve as social hubs, offering retirees the opportunity to make new friends and engage with their communities. Many parks host events, classes and workshops that cater to a wide range of interests, from gardening and fitness to art and history. Taking part in these activities allows retirees to expand their social networks, combat loneliness and foster a sense of belonging.

Exploring local parks and trails can also lead to the discovery of hidden gems and a deeper appreciation of one's community. Retirees may discover historic sites, unique plant species or wildlife habitats that offer a new perspective on their surroundings. These discoveries can spark curiosity, personal growth and a greater sense of connection to the local environment.

Visiting parks and trails can also help retirees develop new hobbies and interests. Activities such as birdwatching, photography and nature journaling can provide a sense of purpose and accomplishment, enriching their retirement experience.

Local parks and trails offer retirees countless opportunities to stay active, engage with their communities and connect with nature. Embracing these natural spaces can lead to improved physical and mental health, new friendships and a deeper understanding of the world around them, all of which contribute to a more fulfilling retirement.

Simple ideas:

- Theme Park Tours: Explore the diversity of local parks by taking a themed tour. Make a list of parks with specific features or themes, such as botanical gardens, historic sites, playgrounds or sculpture parks. This will not only add variety to your visits, but also deepen your appreciation of your local community and its unique offerings.
- Hiking Trail Series: Challenge yourself by completing a series of hiking trails in your area. Start with easier trails and gradually progress to more challenging ones as you build up your stamina and confidence. Completing a trail series can provide a sense of accomplishment and motivate you to explore further.
- Picnic Tours: Turn your park visits into delightful picnic outings. Pack

a lunch, bring a blanket, and choose a different park or scenic spot on a hiking trail for each picnic. This can be an enjoyable way to share the experience with friends or family members while appreciating the beauty of your surroundings.

- Guided Tours and Park Events: Take advantage of guided tours or park events offered by local organizations or park authorities. These events often provide expert insights into the natural, historical, or cultural aspects of the parks and trails. They can also be a great opportunity to meet new people and learn more about the area's hidden gems.
- Nature Journaling: Embrace your creative side by keeping a nature journal during your park and trail visits. Document your observations, thoughts, and feelings, or sketch the landscapes, plants, or animals you encounter. This practice can deepen your connection to nature and provide a lasting record of your outdoor experiences.
- Nature Scavenger Hunt: Create a list of natural items, such as specific plants, rocks, or animal tracks, and challenge yourself or others to find them in the park or along hiking trails.
- Art in the Park: Bring your sketchbook, painting materials, or camera and capture the beauty of your local park or hiking trail through your preferred artistic medium.
- Outdoor Yoga or Tai Chi: Practice yoga or tai chi in a serene park setting, enjoying the calming effects of nature while improving your flexibility and balance.
- Volunteer Opportunities: Join park clean-up events or trail maintenance projects to contribute to the preservation of your local green spaces while connecting with fellow nature enthusiasts.
- Guided Nature Walks: Participate in or organize guided nature walks that focus on local flora, fauna, or geology, providing an educational experience and fostering a deeper appreciation for your surroundings.
- Plant Identification: Learn about the various plant species in your local park or along hiking trails, and educate yourself on their ecological significance, traditional uses, and potential dangers.
- Community Garden: Start or join a community garden in your local park to grow fruits, vegetables, and flowers while fostering social connections and contributing to sustainable urban green spaces.
- Outdoor Book Club: Organize a book club that meets in the park or along a hiking trail, discussing books related to nature, ecology, or local history to deepen your connection to the environment.
- Wildlife Observation: Observe and learn about the wildlife that inhabits your local parks and hiking trails, taking care not to disturb them in their natural habitats.
- Park Bench Meditation: Find a quiet spot in the park to practice meditation or mindfulness exercises, allowing the soothing sounds of nature to enhance your relaxation and focus.

- Playground Workouts: Utilize the playground equipment in local parks for creative and fun bodyweight exercises, transforming your workout routine with a playful twist.
- Sunset or Sunris: Watching: Visit your local park or hiking trail at different times of day to enjoy the beauty of sunrises and sunsets, appreciating the unique lighting and atmosphere they create.
- Seasonal Celebrations: Organize or attend seasonal events in your local parks, such as a spring flower festival, summer picnic, fall foliage walk, or winter snowshoeing excursion.
- Outdoor Movie Nights: Gather friends, family, or neighbors for an outdoor movie night in the park, complete with a portable projector, comfortable seating, and snacks.
- Dog-Friendly Outings: Bring your furry friend along to explore dog-friendly parks and hiking trails, providing exercise and mental stimulation for both you and your pet.

Birdwatching and Wildlife Spotting

Birdwatching and wildlife watching offer retirees a unique opportunity to immerse themselves in nature and observe the incredible biodiversity of their local environment. These activities offer numerous benefits, including physical, mental and social well-being, making them an ideal pastime for those seeking a fulfilling and engaging retirement.

One of the main attractions of birdwatching and wildlife watching is the wide range of species that can be observed in a variety of habitats, from dense forests and wetlands to urban parks and back gardens. Observing these creatures in their natural environment allows retirees to develop a deeper understanding and appreciation of the intricate ecosystems that surround them. In addition, tracking the behaviours, migrations and interactions of different species can inspire a sense of wonder and curiosity that can fuel a lifelong passion for learning and exploration.

In addition to fostering a connection with nature, birdwatching and wildlife watching can also promote physical activity. While some enthusiasts may choose to observe from the comfort of home or a stationary location, others may choose to explore different habitats on foot or by bicycle, hiking along trails or traversing remote areas in search of elusive species. This physical exertion can help maintain cardiovascular health, build stamina and improve overall fitness levels.

Mental health benefits are another important aspect of birdwatching and wildlife watching. The act of observing and identifying species requires concentration and patience, which promotes mindfulness and relaxation. By concentrating on the sights, sounds and behaviours of birds and animals, retirees can temporarily escape the stressors of daily life and find solace in nature. In addition, engaging in these activities can improve cognitive skills such as memory, attention and problem-solving, keeping the mind sharp and alert.

Birdwatching and wildlife watching also provide a social outlet for retirees, offering the chance to meet like-minded people who share their passion for the outdoors. Joining local clubs, taking part in group outings or attending workshops and lectures can help retirees expand their social networks and form lasting friendships. Sharing knowledge, experiences and discoveries with others can enrich the overall experience and foster a sense of belonging to a supportive community.

Bird and wildlife watching can also lead to involvement in citizen science projects and conservation initiatives. By recording observations, contributing to species counts or participating in habitat restoration efforts, retirees can play an important role in preserving biodiversity and supporting scientific research. This sense of purpose and contribution can lead to greater life satisfaction and personal fulfilment.

Birdwatching and wildlife observation offer retirees a diverse and rewarding way to engage with nature and promote physical, mental and social well-being. By developing a passion for observing and understanding the natural world, retirees can cultivate a sense of curiosity, connection and purpose, enriching their retirement experience and overall quality of life.

Birdwatching and wildlife spotting can be done in a variety of locations, depending on the types of species you are interested in observing. Here are some general suggestions for finding great spots to enjoy birdwatching and wildlife spotting:

Local Parks and Nature Reserves: Start by exploring parks and nature reserves in your area. These places often have walking trails, ponds, and designated birdwatching spots where you can observe various bird species and wildlife in their natural habitat.

Wetlands and Marshes: Wetlands, marshes, and swamps are home to a diverse range of birds and wildlife. These areas provide important habitats for waterfowl, wading birds, and many other species that rely on wet environments for nesting and feeding.

Forests and Woodlands: Dense forests and woodlands are great locations for birdwatching and wildlife spotting, as they provide a variety of habitats for different species. Look for trails that traverse various types of terrain, such as meadows, streams, and hills, to maximize your chances of spotting a wide range of birds and wildlife.

Coastal Areas and Beaches: Coastal areas, beaches, and estuaries attract many seabirds, shorebirds, and marine wildlife, such as seals, dolphins, and sea turtles. Visiting these areas during migration seasons can provide exceptional birdwatching opportunities.

Mountains and High-Elevation Areas: Some bird species and wildlife can only be found in high-elevation environments, such as mountains and alpine meadows. These areas can provide unique birdwatching experiences and stunning views of the surrounding landscapes.

National Parks and Wildlife Refuges: Many national parks and wildlife refuges are specifically designed to protect the habitats of various bird and wildlife species. These locations often have dedicated visitor centers, guided tours, and educational programs to enhance your birdwatching and wildlife spotting experience.

Botanical Gardens and Arboretums: Botanical gardens and arboretums often attract a variety of bird species due to their diverse plant life and natural landscapes. These locations can offer a more relaxed and accessible birdwatching experience, especially for those with limited mobility.

Birdwatching Tours and Guided Trips: Joining a guided birdwatching tour or trip can be a great way to explore new locations and learn from experienced birders. These tours are often led by knowledgeable guides who can help you spot and identify different bird species and wildlife.

Birding Festivals and Events: Many communities and organizations host birding festivals and events throughout the year. These events often feature guided birdwatching walks, workshops, and presentations by experts in the field. Participating in these events can provide unique birdwatching opportunities and help you connect with fellow birdwatchers and wildlife enthusiasts.

Gardening for Fun and Health

Gardening offers retirees a rewarding and multifaceted activity that combines the enjoyment of nature with the satisfaction of nurturing and cultivating plants. This pastime provides numerous physical, mental, and social benefits, making it an ideal pursuit for those seeking a fulfilling and healthy retirement.

Physical Benefits of Gardening

Gardening involves a variety of tasks that engage different muscle groups, from digging and planting to pruning and harvesting. These activities help improve strength, flexibility, and coordination, all of which are essential for maintaining overall physical health and independence as we age. Gardening can also provide low-impact cardiovascular exercise, contributing to a healthier heart and improved stamina.

Furthermore, spending time outdoors while gardening exposes retirees to natural sunlight, which aids in the production of vitamin D. This essential nutrient plays a crucial role in maintaining strong bones, supporting the immune system, and regulating mood.

Mental Health Benefits of Gardening

In addition to the physical advantages, gardening offers numerous mental health benefits. Tending to a garden requires focus, patience, and problem-solving skills, which can help keep the mind sharp and engaged. The repetitive nature of many gardening tasks can also foster a sense of mindfulness and relaxation, reducing stress and anxiety levels.

The process of nurturing plants from seed to harvest can provide a sense of accomplishment and purpose, boosting self-esteem and overall life satisfaction. Furthermore, observing the cycles of growth, decay, and renewal in the garden can inspire a deeper connection with nature and a greater appreciation for the resilience and beauty of the natural world.

Social Benefits of Gardening

Gardening also offers opportunities for social interaction and community involvement. Retirees can join local gardening clubs or community gardens, where they can share knowledge, exchange plants, and collaborate on projects with fellow enthusiasts. These connections can help combat loneliness, foster a sense of belonging, and create lasting friendships.

Participating in gardening workshops, plant swaps, or garden tours can also provide retirees with a chance to expand their social networks and deepen their understanding of horticulture. In addition, volunteering for garden-related organizations, such as botanical gardens or conservation groups, can offer a sense of purpose and contribution to the community.

Environmental Benefits of Gardening

By engaging in sustainable gardening practices, retirees can also contribute to the health of the environment. Growing native plants, incorporating organic methods, and promoting biodiversity in the garden can help support local ecosystems and attract beneficial wildlife, such as pollinators and birds. Additionally, growing one's own fruits, vegetables, and herbs can reduce reliance on commercially produced produce, promoting a more sustainable and self-sufficient lifestyle.

Gardening offers retirees a rich and rewarding activity that promotes physical, mental, and social well-being. By cultivating a passion for gardening and connecting with the natural world, retirees can enjoy the numerous health benefits and personal fulfillment this pastime provides, enhancing their overall quality of life during retirement.

Here is a list of gardening ideas that you can consider for your garden:

- Raised Bed Gardens: Build raised beds for your plants to improve drainage, soil quality, and make gardening tasks easier on your back.
- Container Gardening: Grow plants in pots or containers, which is perfect for small spaces, balconies, or patios.
- Vertical Gardening: Utilize vertical space by installing trellises, hanging baskets, or vertical planters to grow climbing plants or vines.
- Herb Garden: Create a dedicated herb garden with a variety of culinary and medicinal herbs, such as basil, parsley, mint, lavender, and rosemary.
- Butterfly and Hummingbird Garden: Plant flowers that attract butterflies, hummingbirds, and other pollinators, such as milkweed, zinnias, and bee balm.
- Rock Garden: Design a rock garden with drought-tolerant plants, succulents, and ornamental grasses, creating an attractive, low-maintenance landscape.
- Perennial Garden: Fill your garden with perennial plants that return year after year, providing color and texture throughout the seasons.
- Vegetable Garden: Grow a variety of vegetables, such as tomatoes, peppers, lettuce, and beans, to enjoy fresh produce from your garden.
- Fruit Garden: Plant fruit trees, berry bushes, or grapevines to enjoy homegrown fruits and create a productive garden.
- Zen Garden: Design a peaceful and tranquil Zen garden with elements such as sand, rocks, and minimalist plantings.
- Pollinator Garden: Create a garden specifically designed to attract and support pollinators like bees, butterflies, and birds by planting native flowering plants and providing nesting habitats.
- Water Garden: Incorporate a water feature, such as a pond or

fountain, and grow aquatic plants like water lilies or water hyacinths.
• Shade Garden: Design a garden specifically for shady areas, featuring shade-tolerant plants like ferns, hostas, and impatiens.
• Sensory Garden: Create a garden that engages all the senses with plants that have interesting textures, fragrances, colors, and sounds.
• Edible Landscaping: Incorporate edible plants, such as fruit trees, berry bushes, and herbs, into your landscape design for a functional and beautiful garden.
• Xeriscaping: Design a low-water garden with drought-tolerant plants and landscaping techniques that conserve water and reduce maintenance.
• Ornamental Grass Garden: Feature a variety of ornamental grasses in your garden for unique textures, colors, and movement.
• Native Plant Garden: Plant native species that are well-adapted to your local climate and soil conditions, promoting biodiversity and attracting local wildlife.
• Cottage Garden: Design a traditional cottage garden with a mix of flowers, herbs, and vegetables, creating a charming and informal atmosphere.
• Children's Garden: Create a dedicated area in your garden for children to learn about plants, grow their own vegetables, and engage with nature.

Fishing and Boating Excursions

Fishing and boating excursions offer retirees the perfect opportunity to combine relaxation, adventure, and connection with nature, making them an ideal pastime for those seeking a fulfilling and diverse retirement experience. These activities provide numerous physical, mental, and social benefits that can significantly enhance the quality of life during one's golden years.

Physical Benefits of Fishing and Boating

Fishing and boating require a range of physical skills and exertion, helping retirees maintain their overall fitness and agility. Casting, reeling, and handling equipment while fishing can improve strength, dexterity, and hand-eye coordination. Boating activities, such as rowing, sailing, or maneuvering a motorboat, engage various muscle groups and can help build endurance and balance.

Spending time outdoors during fishing and boating excursions also exposes retirees to natural sunlight, which supports the production of vitamin D. This essential nutrient is vital for maintaining bone health, boosting the immune system, and regulating mood.

Mental Health Benefits of Fishing and Boating

In addition to the physical benefits, there are many mental health benefits to fishing and boating. The tranquil settings and rhythmic movements of these activities can promote relaxation and reduce stress, providing a welcome escape from the hustle and bustle of everyday life.

Fishing in particular requires patience, concentration and problem-solving skills, which can help keep the mind sharp and engaged. The sense of achievement that comes from catching a fish or mastering a new boating skill can also boost self-esteem and overall life satisfaction.

In addition, immersing oneself in the natural beauty of lakes, rivers or oceans during fishing and boating trips can inspire a deeper appreciation for the environment and foster a sense of connection with the natural world.

Social Benefits of Fishing and Boating

Fishing and boating outings also offer retirees the opportunity to meet like-minded people and make new friends. Joining local fishing or boating clubs, participating in group outings, or attending workshops and seminars can help expand social networks and foster a sense of belonging to a supportive community.

Sharing knowledge, experiences and adventures with others can enrich the overall experience and create lasting memories. Fishing and boating trips can also be enjoyed with family and friends, providing a unique and enjoyable way to bond and create shared experiences.

Conservation and Sustainability in Fishing and Boating

By adopting responsible fishing and boating practices, retirees can contribute to the conservation and sustainability of aquatic ecosystems. Adhering to catch-and-release guidelines, respecting local fishing regulations and using environmentally friendly boating practices can help protect these precious resources for future generations.

Fishing and boating trips offer retirees a diverse and rewarding way to stay active, connect with nature and socialise with others. By embracing the adventure and tranquillity that these activities provide, retirees can cultivate a sense of fulfilment, well-being and purpose, improving their overall quality of life in retirement.

Here is a list of ideas for locations where you can enjoy fishing and boating excursions:

- Local Lakes and Reservoirs: Explore nearby lakes and reservoirs that allow boating and fishing activities. These areas often provide boat rentals, fishing equipment, and picnic areas for a fun day out.
- Rivers and Streams: Visit nearby rivers and streams, where you can enjoy fishing for various species of fish, canoeing, or kayaking through scenic landscapes.
- Coastal Areas and Bays: Head to the coast and explore bays, inlets, and estuaries for fishing and boating excursions. These areas often provide opportunities for saltwater fishing, sailing, and wildlife watching.
- National and State Parks: Many national and state parks offer fishing and boating opportunities in their lakes, rivers, or coastal areas. Be sure to check park regulations and obtain any necessary permits before your excursion.
- Fishing Charters and Guided Tours: Join a fishing charter or guided tour for a professionally organized fishing and boating experience. These excursions often include equipment, instruction, and expert guidance to help you make the most of your day on the water.
- Island Destinations: Plan a trip to an island destination, where you can enjoy fishing and boating excursions in crystal-clear waters and explore stunning marine environments.
- Fishing Resorts and Lodges: Book a stay at a fishing resort or lodge, where you can enjoy a dedicated fishing and boating experience, complete with comfortable accommodations and expert guidance.
- International Fishing Destinations: Travel to renowned international fishing destinations, such as Costa Rica, the Florida Keys, or British Columbia, to experience world-class fishing and boating opportunities.
- River Cruises: Embark on a river cruise, where you can explore picturesque waterways, fish along the banks, and enjoy the comforts of a guided boat tour.
- Canoe and Kayak Trips: Plan a multi-day canoe or kayak trip, where you can paddle through scenic waterways, fish in remote locations, and camp along the shores.
- Marine Protected Areas: Visit marine protected areas or national marine sanctuaries, where you can enjoy responsible fishing and boating activities while admiring the diverse marine life and pristine environments.
- Fly Fishing Destinations: Head to renowned fly fishing destinations, such as Montana or New Zealand, to experience world-class fly fishing excursions and enjoy the beauty of the surrounding landscapes.
- Ice Fishing Adventures: For a unique experience, consider an ice fishing adventure in colder regions, where you can enjoy fishing through the ice and the serene beauty of a frozen landscape.
- Houseboat Rentals: Rent a houseboat for a unique vacation

experience, where you can enjoy fishing and boating excursions right from your floating home.

Geocaching and Treasure Hunting

Geocaching and treasure hunting present retirees with an exciting and unique opportunity to combine their love for exploration, adventure, and the outdoors. These activities offer a multitude of physical, mental, and social benefits, making them ideal pursuits for those seeking a stimulating and fulfilling retirement experience.

Geocaching is a modern-day treasure hunt that utilizes GPS technology to locate hidden containers, called geocaches, placed by fellow enthusiasts. These caches can be found in various locations, ranging from urban settings to remote wilderness areas. The thrill of the hunt, combined with the satisfaction of uncovering hidden treasures, can provide retirees with a sense of excitement, accomplishment, and curiosity.

Treasure hunting, on the other hand, can involve a wide range of activities, from searching for valuable items at flea markets and antique stores to using metal detectors to uncover historical artifacts or buried valuables. These pursuits can spark a passion for history, archaeology, and the thrill of discovery, offering retirees an engaging and rewarding pastime.

One of the primary physical benefits of geocaching and treasure hunting is the increased physical activity they encourage. Retirees often find themselves hiking, climbing, or navigating challenging terrain in search of geocaches or hidden treasures. This physical exertion can help maintain cardiovascular health, build endurance, and improve overall fitness levels.

In addition to promoting physical well-being, geocaching and treasure hunting also offer numerous mental health benefits. The act of problem-solving, deciphering clues, and utilizing navigational skills can help keep the mind sharp and engaged. The focus and determination required for these activities can also foster a sense of mindfulness and relaxation, providing a welcome escape from the stressors of daily life.

Furthermore, the sense of achievement and satisfaction that comes from locating a geocache or unearthing a hidden treasure can boost self-esteem and overall life satisfaction. By continually seeking new challenges and discoveries, retirees can nurture a sense of curiosity, adventure, and personal growth.

Geocaching and treasure hunting also provide ample opportunities for social interaction and connection. Retirees can join local clubs, attend events, or participate in group outings, where they can share their passion for exploration and discovery with fellow enthusiasts. These connections can help combat loneliness, foster a sense of belonging, and create lasting friendships.

Geocaching and treasure hunting can lead to involvement in community projects or conservation initiatives. By hiding and maintaining geocaches, volunteering for archaeological digs, or participating in clean-up efforts, retirees can play a vital role in supporting their local communities and preserving the environment.

Geocaching and treasure hunting offer retirees a captivating and adventurous way to stay active, engage their minds, and connect with others. By embracing the thrill of exploration and discovery, retirees can cultivate a sense of curiosity, accomplishment, and purpose, enhancing their overall quality of life during retirement.

Geocaching and treasure hunting can be enjoyed in various locations, from urban settings to remote natural areas. Here are some ideas for places where you can embark on geocaching and treasure hunting adventures:

- Local Parks and Green Spaces: Start by exploring your local parks, community gardens, and other green spaces, where geocaches are often hidden in creative ways.
- Urban Areas and Cityscapes: Geocaching in urban areas can lead you to discover interesting landmarks, public art installations, or historical sites, making it a fun way to explore your city.
- Hiking Trails and Forests: Hit the hiking trails and explore forests to find geocaches hidden among trees, rocks, and other natural features.
- Beaches and Coastal Areas: Search for geocaches along beaches, coastal paths, and scenic overlooks, while enjoying the beauty of the sea and shoreline.
- National and State Parks: Many national and state parks allow geocaching, giving you the chance to explore protected landscapes and learn about the area's natural and cultural history.
- Historic Sites and Landmarks: Visit historic sites, monuments, and landmarks, where geocaches may be hidden in a way that highlights the site's significance or interesting features.
- Roadside Attractions and Rest Stops: When traveling, look for geocaches at roadside attractions, rest stops, or points of interest along your route, adding an element of adventure to your road trip.
- Small Towns and Rural Areas: Explore small towns and rural areas where geocaches may be hidden in quaint locations, such as old buildings, bridges, or scenic spots.

- Themed Trails and Geotours: Some communities and organizations create themed geocaching trails or geotours, which guide you through a series of geocaches that share a common theme or story.
- Worldwide Geocaching Events: Participate in geocaching events or gatherings, where you can meet fellow enthusiasts, exchange tips, and embark on group geocaching adventures.
- Metal Detecting: For a different type of treasure hunting, try using a metal detector to search for coins, relics, or other hidden treasures at beaches, parks, or historical sites.
- Adventure Racing: Join adventure races or orienteering events that combine geocaching or treasure hunting with other outdoor activities, such as running, biking, or kayaking.
- Scavenger Hunts: Organize a scavenger hunt with friends or family, where participants search for hidden items or clues in a designated area, adding a competitive element to your treasure hunting adventure.
- Letterboxing: Similar to geocaching, letterboxing involves following clues to find hidden boxes containing unique stamps and logbooks, providing another exciting treasure hunting option.

Walking or Hiking Groups

Walking or hiking groups offer retirees a fantastic way to stay active, engage with nature, and connect with others who share similar interests. These groups provide a supportive and inclusive environment, making them an ideal pursuit for those seeking a fulfilling and healthy retirement experience. Participating in walking or hiking groups can lead to numerous physical, mental, and social benefits that significantly enhance retirees' overall quality of life.

Physical Benefits of Walking or Hiking Groups

Walking and hiking are low-impact exercises that can be easily adapted to suit various fitness levels and abilities. Regular participation in walking or hiking groups can help retirees maintain their cardiovascular health, improve balance and coordination, and build strength and endurance. These activities are also beneficial for weight management and can help prevent or manage chronic health conditions, such as diabetes, heart disease, and high blood pressure.

Furthermore, walking or hiking outdoors exposes retirees to natural sunlight, which aids in the production of vitamin D, an essential nutrient for maintaining bone health, supporting the immune system, and regulating mood.

Mental Health Benefits of Walking or Hiking Groups

In addition to the physical advantages, walking or hiking groups provide numerous mental health benefits. Being outdoors and surrounded by nature can help reduce stress levels, promote relaxation, and enhance overall well-being. Studies have shown that spending time in natural environments can improve mood, decrease anxiety, and even increase cognitive function.

The act of walking or hiking itself can also foster a sense of mindfulness and present-moment awareness, as participants focus on their surroundings and the rhythm of their steps. This can lead to a greater sense of inner peace and tranquility, contributing to improved mental health and emotional resilience.

Social Benefits of Walking or Hiking Groups

One of the most significant benefits of joining walking or hiking groups is the opportunity for social interaction and connection. Retirees can meet like-minded individuals, share experiences, and forge new friendships within a supportive and encouraging community. These connections can help combat loneliness, foster a sense of belonging, and create lasting bonds.

Furthermore, walking or hiking groups often organize events, outings, or trips to new destinations, providing retirees with a chance to explore new places and expand their horizons. These adventures can lead to unforgettable experiences and a broader perspective on life.

Engaging in walking or hiking groups can also offer retirees a sense of purpose and contribution, as they can volunteer to lead walks, organize events, or share their knowledge and skills with others. This involvement can lead to increased self-esteem and a greater sense of fulfillment.

Walking or hiking groups provide retirees with a rewarding and supportive way to stay active, engage with nature, and connect with others. By participating in these activities, retirees can cultivate a sense of well-being, adventure, and camaraderie, enhancing their overall quality of life during retirement.

Here is a list of ideas for walking or hiking groups that you can consider joining or creating:

• Nature Walks Group: Organize a group focused on exploring local nature trails, parks, and reserves, while appreciating the beauty of the natural surroundings.

- Urban Explorers: Create a walking group that explores urban areas, discovering interesting landmarks, architecture, and hidden gems within the city.
- Fitness Walkers: Start a group focused on walking for exercise, with members of similar fitness levels and goals, meeting regularly for brisk walks or power walking sessions.
- Birdwatching and Wildlife Walks: Form a group with a shared interest in birdwatching and wildlife spotting, visiting various habitats and observing the local fauna.
- Historical Walks: Organize a group that explores historical sites, landmarks, and neighborhoods, learning about local history and culture along the way.
- Photography Walks: Create a walking group for photography enthusiasts, visiting picturesque locations and practicing photography skills together.
- Dog Walking Group: Start a group for dog owners who enjoy walking their pets in a social setting, visiting dog-friendly parks and trails.
- Family-Friendly Hikes: Organize a group that focuses on family-friendly hikes and walks, with trails suitable for children and parents to enjoy together.
- Senior Walking Group: Create a group catered to seniors who wish to stay active and socialize, planning gentle walks and accessible routes.
- Mindfulness and Meditation Walks: Start a group that combines walking with mindfulness and meditation exercises, promoting mental well-being and relaxation.
- Trail Maintenance and Conservation: Form a group that combines hiking with trail maintenance and conservation efforts, working together to preserve and protect local trails and natural areas.
- Themed Walks and Hikes: Organize a group that focuses on themed walks and hikes, such as visiting waterfalls, exploring caves, or following in the footsteps of famous explorers or authors.
- Night Hikes and Stargazing: Create a group that embarks on night hikes, exploring trails under the moonlight and stargazing together.
- Weekend Hiking Adventures: Start a group that plans weekend hiking trips to nearby national parks, forests, or other scenic destinations.
- Multi-Activity Outdoor Group: Organize a group that combines walking and hiking with other outdoor activities, such as cycling, kayaking, or rock climbing, for a more varied outdoor experience.
- Social Walking Group: Create a walking group focused on socializing, planning leisurely walks with opportunities for conversation and making new friends.
- Women's Walking and Hiking Group: Start a group specifically for women, providing a supportive and empowering environment for female walkers and hikers.

- Volunteer-Led Walking Tours: Join or create a group that participates in volunteer-led walking tours, sharing knowledge and stories about local history, architecture, or other interesting topics.

Beekeeping

Beekeeping is a unique and fascinating opportunity for retirees to engage in a sustainable and fulfilling hobby that benefits both the environment and their well-being. As beekeepers, retirees can immerse themselves in the fascinating world of honey bees, learning about their complex social structure, behaviour and the essential role they play in pollination and the maintenance of biodiversity.

One of the most important benefits of retired beekeeping is the opportunity to contribute to the conservation of honey bees and other pollinators. Honeybee populations are declining worldwide due to factors such as habitat loss, pesticide exposure and disease. By providing a safe and nurturing environment for honey bees, retirees can play an active role in supporting these vital pollinators and promoting environmental sustainability.

In addition to the environmental benefits, beekeeping offers retirees several physical and mental health benefits. The tasks involved in beekeeping, such as inspecting hives, lifting frames and harvesting honey, can help maintain overall fitness, strength and dexterity. In addition, spending time outdoors and engaging in purposeful activity can improve mood, reduce stress levels and promote a sense of well-being.

Beekeeping also offers many opportunities for intellectual stimulation and personal growth. Retirees can increase their knowledge of honey bees, their life cycle and the intricate workings of the hive through research, workshops and hands-on experience. Mastering the art of beekeeping and overcoming challenges can lead to a sense of achievement and self-confidence.

Beekeeping can also be an incredibly rewarding hobby in terms of the tangible products it produces. Retirees can enjoy the fruits of their labour in the form of honey, beeswax and other hive products. These items can be used for personal consumption, shared with family and friends, or even sold, providing a potential source of income or an opportunity to give back to the community.

Beekeeping also offers a wide range of social benefits. Retirees can connect with other beekeepers through local clubs, associations or online forums. These networks provide a supportive community where retirees can share their experience, knowledge and passion for beekeeping. Participation in workshops, conferences and other events can further develop social connections and foster a sense of belonging.

In addition, beekeeping can act as a catalyst for engagement with the wider community. By educating others about the importance of honey bees and pollinators, retirees can raise awareness and inspire others to take action to protect the environment. Sharing their expertise with schools, community groups or garden clubs can give retirees a sense of purpose and contribution.

Beekeeping offers retirees a unique and meaningful way to stay active, keep their minds active and connect with others while contributing to the health of the environment. By embracing the fascinating world of honey bees and the art of beekeeping, retirees can cultivate a sense of purpose, accomplishment and well-being, improving their overall quality of life in retirement.

Here are some ideas to consider when starting or expanding your beekeeping activities:

- Urban beekeeping: Set up an apiary in an urban environment, such as a rooftop or small backyard, to help increase pollination in the city.
- Bee-friendly garden: Plant a variety of flowering plants, shrubs and trees that provide nectar and pollen for your bees throughout the seasons.
- Beekeeping workshops and classes: Attend workshops, classes or join a local beekeeping club to learn more about beekeeping techniques, hive management and honey extraction.
- Honey Varieties: Experiment with different types of honey by strategically placing your hives near certain flowering plants, such as lavender or clover, to influence the flavour of the honey.
- Honeycomb products: In addition to honey, consider producing and selling other bee products such as beeswax, pollen and propolis.
- Hive art: Customise your hives with creative artwork, patterns or colours to make them visually appealing and easily identifiable.
- Beekeeping Equipment: Research and invest in innovative beekeeping equipment, such as hive monitoring systems, to make your beekeeping activities more efficient and manageable.
- Bee hotels: Create bee hotels or nesting habitats for solitary bees, which help with pollination and do not produce honey, to support local bee populations.
- Beekeeping education: Offer beekeeping workshops, demonstrations or classes to the public, schools or community groups to educate others about the importance of bees and the art of beekeeping.

- Honey Tastings and Pairings: Host honey tastings and pairings that showcase the different flavours and textures of your honey with different foods, such as cheeses, fruits and teas.
- Adopt-a-Hive Programs: Develop an adopt-a-hive programme that allows individuals or businesses to sponsor a hive in exchange for regular deliveries of honey and updates on the hive's progress.
- Beekeeping Mentoring: Become a mentor to new beekeepers, offering guidance, advice and support to help them succeed in their beekeeping endeavours.
- Pollinator Conservation: Advocate for pollinator conservation by raising awareness of the importance of bees, the threats they face, and the benefits of bee-friendly practices.
- Bee-themed crafts: Create and sell bee-themed crafts such as beeswax candles, lip balms or honey-based skin care products.
- Beekeeping tourism: Offer tours of your apiary to give visitors an up-close look at the inner workings of a bee colony and the process of honey production.

Mushroom Cultivation

Mushroom growing offers retirees a unique and engaging hobby that combines elements of science, nature and the culinary arts. As a mushroom grower, retirees can explore the diverse and fascinating world of fungi, learning about their biology, growth requirements and the many benefits they provide. Growing mushrooms in retirement can lead to numerous physical, mental and social benefits that enhance overall well-being and quality of life.

One of the main benefits of mushroom growing is the opportunity to produce a fresh and nutritious food source. Many edible mushroom species are rich in vitamins, minerals, antioxidants and other health-promoting compounds. Incorporating home-grown mushrooms into meals can contribute to a balanced and healthy diet, supporting overall health and vitality.

In addition to the nutritional benefits, mushroom growing can provide retirees with several physical and mental health benefits. The tasks involved in mushroom growing, such as preparing substrates, inoculating spawn and harvesting, can help maintain general fitness, strength and dexterity. Engaging in purposeful activity can also improve mood, reduce stress levels and promote a sense of well-being.

Mushroom growing offers retirees many opportunities for intellectual stimulation and personal growth. Retirees can increase their knowledge of mushrooms, their growth requirements and cultivation techniques through research, workshops and hands-on experience. Experimenting with different species and growing methods can foster a sense of curiosity and excitement, as well as a sense of accomplishment and self-confidence.

Mushroom growing offers retirees many opportunities for intellectual stimulation and personal growth. Retirees can increase their knowledge of mushrooms, their growth requirements and cultivation techniques through research, workshops and hands-on experience. Experimenting with different species and growing methods can foster a sense of curiosity and excitement, as well as a sense of accomplishment and self-confidence.

In addition, mushroom growing can yield a variety of tangible products such as medicinal extracts, dyes and even materials for art projects. These items can be used for personal enjoyment, shared with family and friends, or even sold, providing a potential source of income or a means of giving back to the community.

Mushroom growing also offers a wide range of social benefits. Retirees can connect with other mushroom enthusiasts through local clubs, associations or online forums. These networks provide a supportive community where retirees can share their experience, knowledge and passion for mushroom growing. Attending workshops, conferences and other events can further strengthen social ties and foster a sense of belonging.

Mushroom growing can act as a catalyst for engagement with the wider community. By educating others about the fascinating world of mushrooms and their many benefits, retirees can raise awareness and inspire others to take an interest in mushroom growing. Sharing their expertise with schools, community groups or garden clubs can give retirees a sense of purpose and contribution.

Offers retirees a unique and rewarding way to stay active, keep their minds active and connect with others while enjoying the fruits of their labour. By embracing the fascinating world of fungi and the art of mushroom growing, retirees can cultivate a sense of purpose, accomplishment and well-being, enhancing their overall quality of life in retirement.

Here are some ideas to consider when starting or expanding your mushroom cultivation activities:

- Grow Different Varieties: Experiment with cultivating different types of mushrooms, such as oyster, shiitake, lion's mane, or maitake, to diversify your production and appeal to various tastes.

- Indoor Mushroom Growing: Set up an indoor growing environment, such as a grow tent or repurposed room, where you can control temperature, humidity, and light to optimize mushroom growth.
- Outdoor Mushroom Logs: Inoculate hardwood logs with mushroom spawn, and grow mushrooms in a shady, moist area of your garden or property.
- Mushroom Kits: Produce and sell mushroom growing kits, which include pre-inoculated substrate and instructions, to help others start their own home mushroom cultivation.
- Edible Landscaping: Incorporate mushroom cultivation into your landscape design by growing mushrooms in woodchip beds, straw bales, or logs throughout your garden.
- Mycoremediation: Utilize the power of mushrooms to break down pollutants and toxins in contaminated soil, helping to restore and rejuvenate the environment.
- Mushroom Foraging Tours: Offer guided mushroom foraging tours, teaching participants how to safely identify and harvest wild mushrooms in local forests or natural areas.
- Workshops and Classes: Teach mushroom cultivation workshops or classes, sharing your knowledge and experience with others interested in growing their own mushrooms.
- Gourmet and Medicinal Mushrooms: Focus on cultivating gourmet and medicinal mushrooms, which can have high market value and potential health benefits.
- Mushroom-Based Products: Develop and sell mushroom-based products, such as dried mushrooms, mushroom powders, tinctures, or supplements, to diversify your offerings.
- Mushroom Art: Create and sell mushroom-inspired art or crafts, such as mushroom sculptures, paintings, or jewelry, to showcase your passion for fungi.
- Sustainable Mushroom Farming: Employ sustainable practices in your mushroom cultivation, such as using locally sourced or recycled materials for substrates and minimizing waste.
- Mycology Research: Partner with local universities or research institutions to conduct mycology research, advancing knowledge about mushroom cultivation and applications.
- Mushroom Festivals and Events: Participate in or organize local mushroom festivals and events, showcasing your cultivated mushrooms and connecting with fellow mushroom enthusiasts.

TRAVEL AND ADVENTURE

Travel and adventure during retirement offer an unparalleled opportunity to explore the world, embrace new experiences, and enrich your life. With the luxury of time and freedom from daily responsibilities, retirees can indulge in their wanderlust and create lasting memories.

One of the greatest aspects of travel and adventure during retirement is the chance to truly immerse oneself in different cultures and landscapes. Whether it's through road trips across the country, cruising the high seas, or discovering hidden gems in your own city, there are countless ways to experience the beauty and diversity of our planet. By venturing beyond familiar surroundings, retirees can gain new perspectives, appreciate different ways of life, and foster a deeper understanding of the world.

Another rewarding aspect of travel during retirement is the opportunity for personal growth and development. Exploring new destinations and participating in unique activities can help retirees learn new skills, challenge themselves, and push beyond their comfort zones. In addition, travel can provide mental and emotional stimulation, keeping the mind sharp and promoting overall well-being.

Travel and adventure also present the chance to connect with others and build lasting relationships. Whether it's through group travel adventures, educational and cultural tours, or volunteering abroad, retirees can form bonds with fellow travelers and locals alike. These connections can enrich their lives, providing support and camaraderie during their journeys.

For many retirees, travel and adventure also offer a sense of purpose and fulfillment. Volunteering abroad or participating in conservation efforts allows retirees to give back to the global community while experiencing new cultures. Furthermore, exploring national parks and UNESCO World Heritage Sites can inspire a greater appreciation for the natural world and the importance of preserving our planet's diverse ecosystems and cultural heritage.

Travel and adventure during retirement are about embracing life's possibilities and making the most of the time and freedom available. By venturing beyond the familiar, engaging with new experiences, and connecting with others, retirees can create a fulfilling and memorable chapter in their lives, filled with discovery, growth, and joy.

Road Trips Across the Country

Cross-country road trips are an incredible way to explore the diverse landscapes, attractions and cultures your country has to offer, all at your own pace. There's something magical about hitting the open road, with the freedom to choose your own path and create your own adventure as you leave the familiar behind for the excitement of the unknown.

On a road trip, you have the opportunity to visit iconic landmarks and attractions, as well as discovering lesser-known gems that might otherwise have been overlooked. This sense of exploration and discovery can be invigorating, giving you a fresh perspective on the places you visit and a deeper appreciation for the unique beauty and history of your country.

Road trips are also a fantastic way to connect with local people and their culture. By stopping in small towns and cities along the way, you can immerse yourself in the local way of life, sampling local cuisine, attending local events and learning about the history and traditions that shape the community. These interactions can lead to lasting memories and a more meaningful travel experience.

The flexibility of road trips allows you to tailor your adventure to your own interests and preferences. You can plan your route around specific themes, such as scenic drives, historic landmarks or national parks, and adjust your itinerary along the way based on new discoveries or recommendations from fellow travellers. This level of personalisation ensures that your journey is truly unique and reflects your passions and curiosities.

One of the most rewarding aspects of road trips is the chance to experience the diverse natural beauty of your country. From stunning coastal vistas to majestic mountains, dense forests to rolling plains, road trips offer a front row seat to the breathtaking scenery and awe-inspiring landscapes that define your nation. These experiences can inspire a greater appreciation for the environment and the importance of preserving these natural treasures for future generations.

Cross-country road trips offer a rich and immersive travel experience that combines adventure, exploration and personal growth. With the freedom to create your own itinerary and the opportunity to discover the hidden beauty of your country, road trips can be a truly memorable way to spend your retirement, creating memories that will last a lifetime.

Here are some ideas for road trips across the country:

- Coastal Drives: Experience the beauty of the coastline by taking a drive along famous coastal routes, such as California's Pacific Coast Highway, Australia's Great Ocean Road, or South Africa's Garden Route.
- Historic Routes: Travel back in time by following historic routes, like Route 66 in the United States, the Romantic Road in Germany, or the Silk Road in Asia.
- Scenic Byways: Discover breathtaking landscapes by driving along designated scenic byways, such as the Blue Ridge Parkway in the United States, the Icefields Parkway in Canada, or the Ring Road in Iceland.
- National Parks: Plan a road trip to visit multiple national parks, allowing you to experience the diverse natural beauty and outdoor activities that these protected areas have to offer.
- Wine and Culinary Tours: Design a road trip around renowned wine regions or culinary hotspots, sampling local cuisine and beverages while learning about the area's food and drink culture.
- Cultural and Heritage Tours: Create a road trip itinerary focused on exploring the cultural and historical landmarks of your country, such as UNESCO World Heritage Sites, ancient ruins, or significant battlefields.
- Music and Arts: Design a road trip around the music and arts scene, visiting cities known for their vibrant music culture, art galleries, or museums, and attending concerts, festivals, or performances along the way.
- Roadside Attractions: Plan a road trip centered on quirky and unique roadside attractions, such as unusual landmarks, roadside art installations, or kitschy tourist spots.
- Wildlife and Nature: Craft a road trip itinerary that includes stops at wildlife reserves, nature parks, or birdwatching spots, providing opportunities to observe and appreciate the local flora and fauna.
- Adventure and Sports: Organize a road trip focused on adventure and outdoor sports, such as hiking, cycling, or white-water rafting, stopping at various destinations offering these activities.
- Literary and Film Locations: Plan a road trip around locations that have inspired famous books or movies, visiting sites that have been featured in popular novels, films, or TV series.
- Themed Road Trips: Create a road trip based on a specific theme, such as lighthouses, covered bridges, or ghost towns, focusing on visiting related attractions and landmarks.

Discovering Hidden Gems in Your Own City

Discovering hidden gems in your own city offers an exciting opportunity to reconnect with your surroundings and appreciate the beauty and uniqueness of the place you call home. Often, we take our local environment for granted, overlooking the wealth of experiences and attractions that lie right on our doorstep. Venturing out to explore your city with fresh eyes can help you uncover a new world of wonder, history, and culture.

One of the joys of discovering hidden gems in your city is that you don't have to travel far to experience the thrill of exploration and adventure. You can start by wandering through lesser-known neighborhoods or areas you haven't visited before, allowing yourself to be guided by curiosity and serendipity. As you walk, you may stumble upon quaint cafes, beautiful parks, or vibrant street art that you never knew existed.

Another benefit of exploring your city is the opportunity to delve deeper into its history and heritage. You can visit small, local museums or galleries, attend talks or guided tours, and learn about the people, events, and traditions that have shaped your city's unique identity. This newfound knowledge can give you a greater appreciation for your city and its roots.

Discovering the hidden gems in your city can also introduce you to new experiences and hobbies. You might discover a hidden park that's perfect for birdwatching, a tucked-away bookstore that offers fascinating reads, or a community centre where you can take dance or art classes. These discoveries can enrich your life and open up new avenues for personal growth and fulfilment.

As you explore your city, you can also make meaningful connections with your local community. By patronising local businesses, attending neighbourhood events and engaging with other residents, you can foster a sense of belonging and contribute to the vibrancy of your city. These relationships can have a lasting impact, creating a stronger sense of community and camaraderie.

Discovering the hidden gems in your city can also inspire you to become an ambassador for your local area. As you uncover the treasures your city has to offer, you can share your knowledge and enthusiasm with friends, family and visitors, encouraging them to explore and appreciate the wonders of your city as well.

Taking the time to discover the hidden gems in your own city can be a rewarding and enriching experience. By venturing beyond the familiar and embracing the spirit of exploration, you can deepen your connection to your local environment, learn about its history and culture, and uncover a world of experiences and opportunities that can enrich your life and sense of community.

Here are some ideas for discovering hidden gems in your own city:

- City Parks and Gardens: Explore the lesser-known parks and gardens in your city, seeking out hidden trails, tranquil ponds, or beautifully manicured gardens.
- Local Museums and Art Galleries: Visit small, local museums or art galleries to discover the history and culture of your city, and view exhibits that showcase local artists and artisans.
- Historic Buildings and Architecture: Take a walking tour of your city's historic buildings and architecture, learning about the unique styles, materials, and techniques used in the construction of these landmarks.
- Neighborhood Markets and Shops: Visit neighborhood markets, shops, and cafes to discover local artisans and producers, and sample regional foods and beverages.
- Hidden Cafes and Bars: Seek out hidden cafes and bars, tucked away in alleys, basements, or backstreets, and enjoy a quiet drink or bite to eat in a cozy and intimate atmosphere.
- Street Art and Murals: Explore your city's vibrant street art scene, discovering murals and installations that reflect the local culture, history, and values.
- Unique Events and Festivals: Attend unique and offbeat events and festivals in your city, such as a local music festival, a street fair, or a food truck rally.
- Hidden Trails and Pathways: Take a walk or bike ride on the less traveled trails and pathways in your city, discovering scenic vistas, hidden waterfalls, or natural habitats.
- Community Centers and Classes: Sign up for classes or workshops at your local community center, learning new skills, and meeting new people.
- Historic Cemeteries and Monuments: Explore the historical significance of your city's cemeteries and monuments, learning about the lives and contributions of notable residents and important figures in your city's history.

Cruising the High Seas

Cruising the high seas offers an unparalleled opportunity to relax, unwind and explore the world's most beautiful destinations, all while enjoying the luxurious amenities and services of a world-class cruise ship. Whether you're looking for adventure, romance or relaxation, cruising the high seas is an experience like no other.

One of the greatest benefits of cruising is the ability to visit multiple destinations in one trip, without the hassle of packing and unpacking. As you sail from port to port, you can discover new cultures, experience unique activities and marvel at the stunning natural beauty of the world's oceans and coastlines.

Cruising also offers an escape from the stresses of everyday life, with a wide range of on-board activities and amenities designed to ensure your comfort and enjoyment. From fine dining and spa treatments to fitness centres and live entertainment, cruise ships offer something for everyone, making it easy to relax and recharge.

Another benefit of cruising is the opportunity to socialise with other travellers and make new friends. Whether you're travelling alone, with a partner or in a group, cruising allows you to meet new people from all over the world, bond over shared experiences and create lasting memories.

Cruising the high seas also offers the chance to take part in unique and adventurous activities. From snorkelling and scuba diving to zip-lining and rock climbing, cruise ships offer a variety of exciting excursions and activities that allow you to explore the world in new and exciting ways.

Cruising also offers the chance to embrace a slower pace of life, allowing you to unplug from technology and enjoy the simple pleasures of the present moment. Watching the sunrise or sunset from the deck of a cruise ship, feeling the sea breeze on your face and listening to the sound of the waves can be a transformative and rejuvenating experience.

Cruising the high seas is a unique and unforgettable experience, offering the chance to explore the world, relax and recharge, and connect with other travellers. Whether you're looking for adventure, romance or relaxation, cruising has something for everyone, allowing you to create lasting memories and embrace the beauty and wonder of the world's oceans and coastlines.

Here are some ideas for cruising the high seas:

- Caribbean Islands: Cruise the Caribbean and visit exotic islands known for their pristine beaches, lush rainforests and vibrant cultures.
- Mediterranean: Explore the Mediterranean, stopping at iconic destinations such as the Greek Islands, the Italian Riviera and the French Riviera.
- Alaska: Embark on a scenic cruise to Alaska, taking in the majestic glaciers, fjords and wildlife of the northern wilderness.
- Pacific Islands: Visit the South Pacific and cruise to destinations such as Hawaii, Tahiti or Fiji, enjoying the beauty of turquoise waters and tropical landscapes.

- Norwegian Fjords: Sail the Norwegian Fjords and take in the breathtaking scenery of towering cliffs, cascading waterfalls and tranquil fjords.
- Northern Europe: Cruise Northern Europe, visiting charming cities such as Copenhagen, Stockholm or St. Petersburg and exploring the region's history and culture.
- Transatlantic: Cross the Atlantic on a transatlantic cruise, experiencing the vastness and beauty of the open sea while enjoying the luxurious amenities on board.
- Around the World: Circumnavigate the globe on an around-the-world cruise, visiting multiple continents and cultures in a single voyage.
- Antarctica: Cruise to Antarctica and experience the pristine beauty of the world's southernmost continent and observe the incredible wildlife that calls it home.
- River Cruises: Experience a river cruise, sailing along iconic waterways such as the Nile, Danube or Amazon, exploring the unique cultures and landscapes of the regions.
- Wildlife expeditions: Join a wildlife expedition cruise and explore some of the world's most remote and biodiverse regions, spotting rare and exotic wildlife.
- Music and Art: Cruise to destinations renowned for their music and arts scenes, such as New Orleans, New York or Paris, and attend concerts, festivals or performances on board and ashore.
- Luxury Cruises: Indulge in luxury cruising and experience the finest cuisine, accommodations and amenities, as well as personalised service and attention to detail.
- Family Cruises: Plan a family-friendly cruise with activities and amenities designed for all ages, such as water parks, kids' clubs and family-friendly shore excursions.
- Culinary Cruises: Embark on a culinary cruise and sample local foods and wines, attend cooking classes and demonstrations, and visit local markets and restaurants.
- Expedition Cruises: Join an expedition cruise to explore remote and off-the-beaten-path destinations and participate in outdoor activities such as kayaking, hiking or snorkelling.
- Health and Wellness: Focus on health and wellness on a cruise with amenities and activities such as yoga classes, fitness centres and healthy cuisine.
- Photography Cruises: Join a photography cruise and learn from professional photographers as you capture stunning images of landscapes, wildlife and cultural landmarks.
- Solo Travel Cruises: Join other solo travellers on a Solo Travel Cruise and participate in social activities and shore excursions designed for independent travellers.

Exploring National Parks and UNESCO World Heritage Sites

Exploring national parks and UNESCO World Heritage Sites is a breathtaking experience that allows you to immerse yourself in the beauty and wonder of the natural world and the rich history and culture of humanity. These sites are carefully selected for their outstanding universal value and are recognized as some of the most significant and extraordinary places on Earth.

National parks offer an opportunity to experience the beauty of nature in all its forms, from towering mountains and vast deserts to pristine lakes and lush rainforests. Exploring these parks allows you to disconnect from the stresses of modern life and reconnect with the natural world, immersing yourself in its wonders and exploring the diverse ecosystems and habitats that make up our planet.

UNESCO World Heritage Sites offer a chance to delve into the rich history and culture of humanity, and discover the stories and traditions that have shaped our world. These sites are chosen for their exceptional value to humanity and offer a glimpse into the creativity, innovation, and spirit of our ancestors.

Exploring these sites allows you to experience a sense of awe and wonder, as you witness the stunning architecture, artwork, and cultural traditions that have been passed down through the generations. From ancient ruins and medieval castles to iconic landmarks and historic cities, UNESCO World Heritage Sites offer a window into the beauty and complexity of human civilization.

In addition to their aesthetic and cultural value, national parks and UNESCO World Heritage sites provide a range of benefits to individuals and society. These sites offer opportunities for outdoor recreation and adventure, including hiking, camping, bird-watching and other activities that promote physical and mental well-being. They also attract visitors from around the world, contributing to local economies and supporting jobs and businesses in nearby communities.

Finally, exploring national parks and UNESCO World Heritage Sites can foster a sense of connection and responsibility for our natural and cultural heritage, inspiring us to be better stewards of the earth and its people. By engaging with these sites, we can deepen our understanding of the interconnectedness of all things and recognise the importance of preserving our planet's natural and cultural treasures for future generations.

Exploring National Parks and UNESCO World Heritage Sites is a transformative and enriching experience, allowing us to connect with the natural world and human civilisation in a profound way. Whether you're looking for adventure, beauty or cultural enrichment, these sites offer a chance to explore the wonders of our world and appreciate the value and diversity of life on Earth.

Ideas for exploring national parks and UNESCO World Heritage Sites:

National Parks:
• Yosemite National Park, California, USA
• Yellowstone National Park, Wyoming, USA
• Banff National Park, Alberta, Canada
• Torres del Paine National Park, Patagonia, Chile
• Kruger National Park, South Africa
• Serengeti National Park, Tanzania
• Grand Canyon National Park, Arizona, USA
• Rocky Mountain National Park, Colorado, USA
• Plitvice Lakes National Park, Croatia
• Jiuzhaigou National Park, China
• Uluru-Kata Tjuta National Park, Australia
• Zion National Park, Utah, USA
• Glacier National Park, Montana, USA
• Mount Rainier National Park, Washington, USA
• Acadia National Park, Maine, USA
• Glacier Bay National Park and Preserve, Alaska, USA
• Bryce Canyon National Park, Utah, USA
• Zion National Park, Utah, USA
• Grand Teton National Park, Wyoming, USA
• Rocky Mountain National Park, Colorado, USA
• Olympic National Park, Washington, USA
• Denali National Park and Preserve, Alaska, USA
• Kenai Fjords National Park, Alaska, USA
• Joshua Tree National Park, California, USA
• Acadia National Park, Maine, USA
• Everglades National Park, Florida, USA
• Arches National Park, Utah, USA
• Canyonlands National Park, Utah, USA
• Great Smoky Mountains National Park, Tennessee and North Carolina, USA
• Yellowstone National Park, Wyoming, Montana, and Idaho, USA

UNESCO World Heritage Sites:

- Machu Picchu, Peru
- Angkor Wat, Cambodia
- Taj Mahal, India
- Petra, Jordan
- Great Barrier Reef, Australia
- Stonehenge, United Kingdom
- Pompeii, Italy
- The Alhambra, Spain
- The Great Wall of China, China
- The Colosseum, Italy
- Old City of Dubrovnik, Croatia
- Historic Centre of Vienna, Austria
- Wieliczka Salt Mine, Poland
- Redwood National and State Parks, California, USA
- Hiroshima Peace Memorial, Japan
- The Great Barrier Reef, Australia
- The Acropolis, Greece
- The Tower of London, United Kingdom
- The Historic Centre of Florence, Italy
- The Taj Mahal, India
- The Old City of Jerusalem, Israel
- The Great Wall of China, China
- The Pyramids of Giza, Egypt
- The Galapagos Islands, Ecuador
- The Historic Centre of Krakow, Poland
- The Historic City of Ayutthaya, Thailand
- The Historic Centre of Salvador de Bahia, Brazil
- The Caves of Lascaux, France
- The Giant's Causeway, United Kingdom
- Giuliet and Romeo, Verona, Italy

Embarking on Solo or Group Travel Adventures

Embarking on solo or group travel adventures can be a transformative and exhilarating experience that allows you to explore new destinations, meet new people, and challenge yourself in new ways. Whether you're seeking adventure, relaxation, or cultural enrichment, solo or group travel can provide a wealth of opportunities to discover the world and discover yourself.

Solo travel offers the chance to venture out on your own, free from the constraints of schedules, agendas, and companions. You have the freedom to choose where to go, what to do, and how to spend your time, and can connect more deeply with the places you visit and the people you meet. Solo travel can also be a chance to challenge yourself, to step outside your comfort zone and explore new cultures and perspectives, and to discover strengths and abilities you never knew you had.

Group travel, on the other hand, provides the opportunity to connect with like-minded individuals and share the experience of discovery and adventure. Whether you join a guided tour, a volunteer group, or a travel club, group travel offers the chance to learn from others, make new friends, and enjoy the safety and support of a community. Group travel can also be a chance to learn from experts, to gain insights into local cultures and traditions, and to deepen your appreciation for the world and its diversity.

Both solo and group travel adventures offer a range of benefits, including personal growth, self-discovery, cultural enrichment, and adventure. They can also provide opportunities for physical and mental rejuvenation, as you engage in activities such as hiking, biking, yoga, or meditation, and connect with the natural world. Whether you're traveling solo or with a group, remember to embrace the experience fully, take in the beauty and wonder of your surroundings, and allow yourself to be transformed by the journey.

Embarking on solo or group travel adventures can be a life-changing experience, allowing you to discover the world and yourself in new ways. Whether you're seeking adventure, relaxation, or cultural enrichment, solo or group travel can provide a wealth of opportunities to explore the world, connect with others, and deepen your understanding and appreciation of our planet and its people. So go ahead, take the plunge, and discover the joys of solo or group travel adventures!

Here are some ideas for solo or group travel adventures:

- Trekking in the Himalayas, Nepal
- Backpacking through Europe
- Road tripping across the United States
- Scuba diving in the Great Barrier Reef, Australia
- Cycling the Silk Road, Central Asia
- Hiking the Inca Trail to Machu Picchu, Peru
- Camping in the Sahara Desert, Morocco
- Exploring the ancient ruins of Angkor Wat, Cambodia
- Volunteering in a wildlife sanctuary in South Africa
- Surfing and yoga retreat in Bali, Indonesia
- Wildlife safari in Tanzania
- Cultural immersion in Japan
- Rock climbing in Yosemite National Park, USA
- Photography tour in Iceland
- Skiing in the Swiss Alps
- Sailing the Greek Islands
- Exploring the Amazon rainforest, Brazil
- Spa and wellness retreat in Thailand
- Wine tasting in Tuscany, Italy
- Learning Spanish in Costa Rica
- Culinary tour in France
- Spiritual retreat in India
- Hot air balloon ride over Cappadocia, Turkey
- Whale watching in Alaska, USA
- Glacier hiking in New

Zealand
- Motorcycle tour of Vietnam
- Surf and beach adventure in Costa Rica
- Trekking the Camino de Santiago, Spain
- Snowboarding in Japan
- Hiking the Appalachian Trail, USA
- Trekking in the Himalayas, Nepal
- Backpacking through Europe
- Road tripping across the United States
- Scuba diving in the Great Barrier Reef, Australia
- Cycling the Silk Road, Central Asia
- Hiking the Inca Trail to Machu Picchu, Peru
- Camping in the Sahara Desert, Morocco
- Exploring the ancient ruins of Angkor Wat, Cambodia
- Volunteering in a wildlife sanctuary in South Africa
- Surfing and yoga retreat in Bali, Indonesia
- safari in Tanzania
- Cultural immersion in Japan
- Rock climbing in Yosemite National Park, USA
- Photography tour in Iceland
- Skiing in the Swiss Alps
- Sailing the Greek Islands
- Exploring the Amazon rainforest, Brazil
- Spa and wellness retreat in Thailand
- Wine tasting in Tuscany, Italy
- Learning Spanish in Costa Rica
- Culinary tour in France
- Spiritual retreat in India

- Hot air balloon ride over Cappadocia, Turkey
- Whale watching in Alaska, USA
- Glacier hiking in New Zealand
- Motorcycle tour of Vietnam
- Surf and beach adventure in Costa Rica
- Trekking the Camino de Santiago, Spain
- Snowboarding in Japan
- Hiking the Appalachian Trail, USA
- Dog sledding in Lapland, Finland
- Backpacking through Southeast Asia
- Rafting the Grand Canyon, Arizona, USA
- Wildlife and nature photography tour in Yellowstone National Park, USA
- Spiritual retreat in Bali, Indonesia
- Cultural tour of ancient Egypt
- Snowshoeing in the Swiss Alps
- Hiking the Overland Track in Tasmania, Australia
- Wine and food tour in Napa Valley, California, USA
- Surfing and beach camping in Portugal
- Kayaking through the fjords of Norway
- Volunteering at a sea turtle conservation project in Costa Rica
- Mountain biking in Moab, Utah, USA
- Wildlife and nature photography tour in the Pantanal, Brazil

- Learning to cook Thai food in Chiang Mai, Thailand
- Adventure and nature tour in Patagonia, Argentina and Chile
- Cultural and historical tour of Rome, Italy
- Visiting the historical sites of Jerusalem, Israel
- Safari and wildlife photography tour in the Maasai Mara, Kenya
- Skiing and snowboarding in Whistler, Canada

Volunteering Abroad: Combining Travel and Service

Volunteering abroad is a great way to combine your love of travel with your desire to make a positive impact on the world. Whether you're interested in environmental conservation, community development, healthcare or education, there are countless opportunities to volunteer abroad and make a meaningful difference to the lives of others.

Volunteering abroad allows you to immerse yourself in a new culture, learn about local customs and traditions, and build relationships with people from different backgrounds. It is also an opportunity to develop new skills, gain valuable work experience and enhance your CV. In addition, volunteering abroad can be a transformative personal experience, allowing you to develop a greater sense of empathy and compassion and to connect more deeply with the world around you.

There are a variety of volunteering opportunities available, from short-term projects lasting a few weeks to long-term assignments that can last several months or even years. Some popular types of volunteering abroad include

- Teaching English or other subjects in schools or community centres
- Working on environmental projects such as reforestation, wildlife conservation or sustainable agriculture
- Providing health care or medical services in hospitals or clinics
- Building or repairing homes, schools, or other infrastructure in underserved communities
- Helping with disaster relief or refugee assistance programmes
- Helping to develop and implement educational programmes or community initiatives
- Providing care and support to vulnerable groups such as children, the elderly or people with disabilities.

If you're considering volunteering abroad, it's important to research and choose a reputable organisation that matches your values and interests. You should also consider factors such as location, living arrangements and programme costs, and be prepared to adapt to new and potentially challenging situations.

Volunteering abroad can be a deeply rewarding and transformative experience, allowing you to combine travel and service in a meaningful way. By choosing a volunteering opportunity that matches your interests and values, you can make a positive difference to the lives of others while gaining valuable personal and professional experience. So why not take the plunge and embark on a volunteering adventure that can change your life and the lives of others for the better?

Here are some more local volunteering ideas:

- Tutoring or mentoring children in your community.
- Volunteering at a local animal shelter or wildlife sanctuary.
- Assisting with environmental conservation efforts in your area, such as cleaning up parks or beaches.
- Providing assistance to the elderly or people with disabilities, such as running errands or offering companionship.
- Helping out at a local food bank or soup kitchen.
- Volunteering at a hospital or hospice care center, providing comfort and support to patients and their families.
- Participating in a community gardening project, helping to grow fresh produce for those in need.
- Supporting local disaster relief efforts, such as providing aid and supplies to victims of wildfires, hurricanes, or other natural disasters.
- Assisting with youth sports programs, such as coaching or refereeing.
- Volunteering at a community center or after-school program, offering support and guidance to children and teens.
- Participating in a beach cleanup or river restoration project.
- Providing support and care for individuals with mental health or substance abuse issues.
- Helping to build or renovate affordable housing for low-income families.
- Assisting with disaster preparedness efforts, such as organizing emergency supply kits or offering first-aid training.
- Volunteering at a community theater or arts organization, helping to promote and produce local cultural events.
- Supporting literacy and education programs, such as tutoring or organizing book drives.
- Assisting with community fundraising efforts, such as organizing benefit concerts or charity walks.

- Participating in a citizen science project, helping to collect data on environmental or wildlife issues.
- Providing administrative or marketing support to a local non-profit organization.
- Serving as a volunteer mentor for at-risk youth or individuals who are re-entering society after incarceration.
- Assisting with disaster relief efforts abroad, such as providing medical care or rebuilding infrastructure.
- Volunteering at a local library, helping to organize events or assisting with research projects.
- Serving as a volunteer mentor or tutor for immigrants or refugees, helping them to learn English and adjust to life in a new country.
- Assisting with environmental restoration efforts, such as planting trees or restoring wetlands.
- Providing legal assistance to low-income individuals through pro bono work or volunteering at a legal aid clinic.
- Serving as a volunteer coach or referee for community sports teams, helping to promote physical activity and teamwork.
- Participating in a community garden or urban farming project, helping to grow fresh produce for local residents.
- Assisting with disaster response and relief efforts internationally, such as rebuilding homes or providing emergency supplies.
- Providing care and support to individuals with chronic illnesses or disabilities, such as organizing activities or providing transportation.
- Volunteering at a local museum or historical society, helping to preserve and promote local history and culture.

Participating in Educational and Cultural Tours

Taking part in educational and cultural tours can be a rewarding and enriching experience, allowing you to explore new places, learn about different cultures and gain a deeper understanding of the world around you. Whether you're interested in history, art, cuisine or music, there are countless educational and cultural tours available to suit a wide range of interests and preferences.

Educational and cultural tours offer the opportunity to visit museums, historical sites and cultural landmarks, and learn about the stories and traditions that have shaped them. They also offer the chance to meet new people from different backgrounds, learn from local experts and guides, and gain a deeper appreciation of the world's diversity.

Some popular types of educational and cultural tours include:

- Art tours: These tours take you to museums, galleries and other cultural institutions to view art and learn about its history and significance.

• Historical tours: These tours focus on the history of a particular place or region, often visiting historical sites, monuments and landmarks.

• Food and wine tours: These tours take you on a culinary journey, allowing you to sample local cuisine and wine while learning about the culture and traditions that have influenced it.

• Music Tours: These tours focus on the music and cultural traditions of a particular location, often including live performances and visits to music-related landmarks.

• Language immersion tours: These tours offer the opportunity to learn a new language while experiencing the culture and traditions of the place where it is spoken.

• Art Tours: Visit world-renowned art museums such as the Louvre in Paris, the Uffizi Gallery in Florence, or the Museum of Modern Art in New York City. Learn about different artistic movements and styles and see some of the world's most famous works of art.

• Historical tours: Explore ancient civilisations in places like Egypt, Greece and Rome. Visit major historical landmarks such as the Great Wall of China, the Colosseum in Rome or the Pyramids of Giza. Learn about the rich history of Europe on a tour of castles and cathedrals.

• Food and wine tours: Taste the local cuisine in countries like Italy, France or Spain. Take a wine tour in California's Napa Valley or explore the vineyards of Tuscany. Discover the spices and flavours of Asia on a food tour in Thailand, Vietnam or India.

• Music tours: Experience the vibrant music scene in cities like New Orleans, Memphis or Nashville. Take a tour of the birthplace of jazz in New Orleans or explore the roots of rock 'n' roll in Memphis. Learn about the influence of music on cultures around the world, from classical music in Vienna to the rhythms of Brazil.

• Language immersion trips: Learn Spanish in Spain or Latin America, or immerse yourself in French language and culture in Paris. Learn Japanese in Tokyo or Mandarin in China.

• Architecture tours: Explore the architectural wonders of cities such as Barcelona, Chicago or Dubai. Visit iconic buildings such as the Gaudi-designed Sagrada Familia in Barcelona, the Willis Tower (formerly the Sears Tower) in Chicago, or the Burj Khalifa in Dubai.

• Literary tours: Tour the homes and neighbourhoods of famous writers such as Shakespeare, Jane Austen and Ernest Hemingway. Visit bookshops and literary landmarks in cities such as Paris, Dublin or Edinburgh.

• Nature tours: Explore the world's natural wonders, such as the Grand Canyon, the Great Barrier Reef or the Amazon rainforest. Learn about the flora and fauna of different regions and discover the importance of

conservation efforts.
- Cultural festivals: Take part in cultural festivals and celebrations around the world, such as Carnival in Rio de Janeiro, the Lantern Festival in China or the Day of the Dead in Mexico. Learn about the traditions and customs that make these events so unique and special.
- Religious Tours: Visit major religious sites and landmarks such as the Vatican in Rome, the Western Wall in Jerusalem or the temples of Kyoto. Learn about the history and significance of different religions and their impact on the world.

When considering educational and cultural tours, it's important to choose a tour that matches your interests and preferences. You should also consider factors such as travel arrangements, itinerary and cost, and be prepared to adapt to new and potentially challenging situations.

Taking part in educational and cultural travel can be a transformative and enriching way to explore new places, learn about different cultures and gain a deeper appreciation of the world around you. Whether you're interested in art, history, food, music or language, there's a tour to suit your interests and preferences. So why not take the opportunity to step out of your comfort zone, immerse yourself in a new culture and embark on an educational and cultural adventure that can broaden your horizons and deepen your understanding of the world?

Exploring the World through Home Exchanges and House Sitting

Exploring the world through home exchange and house sitting can be a great way to travel and experience new cultures without breaking the bank. Home exchange involves swapping homes with someone in another part of the world, while house sitting involves looking after someone's home and pets while they are away. Both options allow travellers to live like the locals and have a more authentic experience than staying in a hotel or resort.

Home exchange and house sitting can offer a number of benefits. Firstly, they can be much more affordable than traditional forms of travel, as there are usually no accommodation costs involved. Travellers can also save money on food and other expenses by cooking meals in the home they are staying in. Home exchange and house sitting can also provide a more personal and unique travel experience, as travellers are able to live like the locals and get a feel for what life is really like in another part of the world.

When participating in a home exchange or house sitting, it's important to be prepared and do your research. Before agreeing to a home exchange, it is important to communicate with the homeowner and establish clear guidelines for the exchange. This should include information about cleaning and maintenance expectations, as well as any specific rules or regulations that need to be followed.

When house sitting, it's important to be responsible and take good care of the home and any pets in your care. This may include feeding and grooming pets, watering plants and ensuring that the home is safe and secure.

Exploring the world through home exchange and house sitting can be a great way to travel and experience new cultures. Whether you're interested in staying in a cosy cabin in the woods, a villa on the beach or a city apartment, there are many opportunities for travellers who are willing to exchange or care for homes. By participating in a home exchange or house sitting, travellers can save money, gain a more authentic travel experience and create memories that will last a lifetime.

Here are some ideas for exploring the world through home exchange and house sitting:

Exchange homes with someone in another part of the world and spend your holiday living like a local. You can explore the local culture, try new foods and get to know the community.

Look after someone's home and pets while they are away. This can be a great way to save money on accommodation while experiencing a new city or country.

Join a work exchange programme where you work in exchange for room and board. This can be a great way to gain work experience and travel at the same time.

Volunteer as a home sitter for an elderly or disabled person, providing companionship and support while gaining travel experience.

Rent a holiday home or apartment and experience life like a local in a different part of the world. You can explore the local culture, try new foods and immerse yourself in the local community.

Join a homeshare programme where you share a home with a local family or individual. This can be a great way to learn about a new culture and experience life as a local.

Swap homes with someone in a different part of the world and experience a new culture without breaking the bank. You can explore local attractions, try new foods and get to know the community.

Stay in a hostel or guesthouse and meet other travellers from all over the world. This can be a great way to make new friends and learn about different cultures.

Rent a houseboat or motorhome and explore a new part of the world from the comfort of your own home. This can be a great way to see the sights and experience the local culture, while enjoying the freedom and flexibility of travelling on your own terms.

Work as a caretaker for a holiday property, looking after the property and its guests in exchange for free or discounted accommodation. This can be a great way to gain work experience and travel at the same time.

Participate in a home exchange programme where you exchange your home with someone in another part of the world for a set period of time. This can be a great way to experience life in another part of the world while saving money on accommodation.

Rent a furnished apartment or house for an extended period and experience life like a local in another part of the world. This can be a great way to immerse yourself in the local culture, learn the language and make new friends.

Volunteer on a farm or in a rural community and experience life in a different part of the world while contributing to a worthwhile cause. This can be a great way to learn about sustainable farming and living off the land, while making a positive impact on the local community.

Join a house sitting network where you can connect with homeowners who need house sitters and find opportunities to travel and explore the world. This can be a great way to build relationships with homeowners and other travellers, and gain valuable travel experience.

Travel and Exploration

Travel and exploration can be an incredibly rewarding and fulfilling experience, offering the opportunity to learn about different cultures, meet new people and see the world from a different perspective. Whether you're travelling alone, with your family or in a group, there are countless ways to explore the world and make unforgettable memories.

One of the most popular forms of travel is sightseeing, which involves visiting famous landmarks, museums and historical sites. This can be a great way to learn about the history and culture of different regions and gain a deeper appreciation of the world around us. From the ancient ruins of Machu Picchu to the modern architecture of Tokyo, there is no shortage of incredible sights to see around the world.

Another popular form of travel is adventure travel, which involves taking part in outdoor activities such as hiking, camping and rock climbing. This can be a great way to challenge yourself physically and mentally, while experiencing the natural beauty of different parts of the world. Whether you're trekking through the Himalayas or kayaking down the Amazon, there's no shortage of adventures around the world.

Another popular form of travel is cultural immersion, which involves living like a local and experiencing the culture of a different region or country. This can involve anything from trying the local cuisine to learning the language and customs of the people who live there. By immersing yourself in another culture, you can gain a deeper understanding of the world and broaden your horizons in ways you never thought possible.

Whatever your travel preferences, there is likely to be an opportunity to travel and explore that offers a unique and enriching experience. By travelling and exploring the world, you can gain new perspectives, meet new people and create memories that will last a lifetime.

Here are some ideas for travel and exploration during retirement:

- Take a cruise around the world, visiting different ports of call and experiencing different cultures and landscapes.
- Embark on a road trip across the country, visiting national parks, historical sites, and other popular tourist destinations.
- Plan a trip to a foreign country where you can immerse yourself in the local culture, try new foods, and explore the sights and sounds of a different part of the world.
- Join a travel group or tour, where you can meet other like-minded travelers and experience the world together.
- Volunteer abroad, combining travel and service to make a positive impact on the world while also gaining valuable travel experience.
- Plan a trip to visit family and friends who live in different parts of the world, reconnecting with loved ones and creating new memories together.
- Visit a region known for its natural beauty, such as the mountains or the coast, and spend time hiking, camping, or exploring the outdoors.

- Attend a cultural event or festival in a different part of the world, immersing yourself in the local traditions and customs.
- Plan a trip to explore historical sites and landmarks, learning about the rich history of different regions and civilizations.
- Take a leisurely train ride through a scenic region, enjoying the views and the relaxation of traveling by train.
- Plan a trip to visit a different part of the world during each season, experiencing the changing landscapes and weather patterns.
- Take a culinary tour of different regions or countries, trying new foods and learning about local cooking traditions.
- Visit a wine region and take a tour of local vineyards, learning about the wine-making process and trying different varieties.
- Plan a trip to explore different national parks, hiking or camping in each one and experiencing the unique natural beauty of each region.
- Join a group tour or volunteer program that focuses on sustainable travel, learning about eco-friendly travel practices and ways to make a positive impact on the environment.
- Take a photography tour, exploring different regions and capturing beautiful images of landscapes, wildlife, and local culture.
- Plan a trip to attend a music or arts festival in a different part of the world, experiencing the local art and culture while also enjoying live performances.
- Take a language immersion course in a foreign country, learning a new language while also experiencing the local culture and making new friends.
- Visit a different region or country for each major holiday, experiencing the unique traditions and celebrations of different cultures.
- Plan a trip to explore different regions of the world known for their natural wonders, such as the Great Barrier Reef or the Amazon rainforest.

CREATIVE PURSUITS WHEN RETIREMENT

Retirement is a time for new beginnings and an opportunity to explore hobbies and interests that may have been put on hold during your career. Engaging in creative activities is an excellent way to spend this new-found free time. Creative activities not only provide a sense of fulfilment, but also improve mental health, cognitive function and overall well-being.

There are many creative pursuits that retirees can explore. One popular activity is painting and drawing. For those who have never picked up a paintbrush or pencil, retirement is an excellent time to explore this artistic outlet. It is an opportunity to try new techniques, experiment with different media and express yourself through the visual arts.

Crafting is another popular creative activity for retirees. There are countless types of crafts to explore, from knitting and crocheting to sewing and embroidery. Crafting is a great way to engage in a relaxing activity while creating something unique and handmade. It is also an excellent way to socialise with others who share similar interests, as many community craft groups exist.

Writing and journaling is another creative activity that retirees can explore. Writing provides a means of self-expression and reflection, which can be particularly beneficial in retirement. Journaling is an excellent way to capture memories and experiences while exploring personal growth and emotional well-being. Many retirees find that writing and journaling provide a sense of purpose and fulfilment.

Pottery and ceramics are also popular creative pursuits for retirees to explore. These activities offer the opportunity to create functional and beautiful objects with your own hands. Pottery and ceramics also involve learning new techniques and tools, which can provide a sense of intellectual stimulation and satisfaction.

Performing arts such as acting, singing and dancing can be a fun and rewarding way to engage in a creative activity in later life. Participation in these activities can improve physical health and mental well-being, and provide an opportunity to socialise with others who share similar interests. Local classes and performances are often available for retirees interested in exploring these activities.

Retirement is an excellent time to explore new hobbies and interests, including creative activities. Engaging in creative activities can provide a sense of purpose, fulfilment and intellectual stimulation. Whether retirees choose to explore painting, crafts, writing, pottery and ceramics, or the performing arts, there is something for everyone.

Painting and Drawing for Beginners

Painting and drawing are two artistic activities that provide an excellent outlet for self-expression and creativity. Not only are these activities enjoyable, but they also offer many benefits to those who engage in them, including improved mental health, cognitive function and overall well-being. Retirement is an excellent time to explore painting and drawing, as it offers the opportunity to develop new skills and create something beautiful.

For beginners, painting and drawing can seem daunting. However, it is important to remember that everyone starts somewhere and with practice anyone can develop their skills. The key to success is to start with the basics and work your way up. For painting, this means learning about colour theory, understanding how to mix colours and becoming familiar with different types of paint and brushes. For drawing, it means learning about proportion, perspective and shading.

One way to get started in painting and drawing is to take a class or workshop. Many communities offer classes specifically for beginners and these can be an excellent way to learn the basics in a supportive environment. Classes offer the opportunity to learn from an experienced teacher, get feedback on your work and meet others with similar interests.

Another way to get started with painting and drawing is to simply start experimenting on your own. Invest in some basic materials, such as paint, brushes and paper, or pencils, erasers and sketchbooks, and start creating. The more you practice, the more comfortable you will become with the techniques and mediums.

Finally, it is important to enjoy the process of painting and drawing, rather than just focusing on the end result. These activities provide an opportunity to express oneself and explore creativity, which can be a rewarding and enjoyable experience in itself. It is important to take time to appreciate the journey and not just focus on the destination.

Painting and drawing are two creative pursuits that can bring many benefits to retirees. While it can be intimidating to start as a beginner, there are many resources available to help individuals develop their skills. By taking classes, practising on their own and embracing the process, retirees can enjoy the many benefits of painting and drawing.

Here are some ideas for painting and drawing projects for beginners in retirement:

• Still life painting: A still life is an excellent way to practice colour mixing, shading and brushwork. Make a simple arrangement of objects, such as fruit or flowers, and try to capture their shape and texture on canvas.
• Landscape drawing: Drawing a landscape is a great way to practise perspective and proportion. Choose a simple scene, such as a park or beach, and try to capture the detail and sense of space.
• Portrait drawing: Drawing a portrait is a great way to practise capturing the human form. Choose a subject, such as a family member or friend, and try to capture their likeness on paper.
• Watercolour painting: Watercolour is a beautiful and forgiving medium, perfect for beginners. Experiment with different colours and techniques such as wet-on-wet and wet-on-dry to create beautiful washes and textures.
• Charcoal drawing: Charcoal is a versatile medium, perfect for creating bold, dramatic drawings. Experiment with different types of charcoal and paper, and try creating both light and dark tones to add depth and contrast to your work.
• Abstract Painting: Abstract painting is an excellent way to express oneself creatively without being constrained by form or representation. Experiment with different colors, shapes, and textures to create a unique and expressive work of art.
• Sketching: Sketching is a great way to improve one's drawing skills and capture the world around us. Take a sketchbook and pencil with you on walks or trips, and try to capture the scenes and objects you encounter.
• Ink Drawing: Ink is a beautiful and versatile medium that can be used for both drawing and painting. Experiment with different types of ink and brushes, and try creating both bold and delicate lines to add interest and texture to your work.

Crafting Your Way to Happiness

Crafting is a wonderful way to spend your retirement years, providing a creative outlet that can bring joy and fulfilment. Engaging in craft activities has been shown to have numerous mental and physical health benefits, such as reducing stress, improving mood and increasing cognitive function. In addition to the health benefits, crafting also provides a sense of accomplishment and can help retirees connect with others who share similar interests.

There are countless types of crafting that retirees can explore, from knitting and crocheting to sewing and embroidery. Crafting is a relaxing activity that can be done alone or in groups, and it provides a sense of purpose and satisfaction in creating something unique and handmade.

One of the benefits of crafting is the opportunity to learn new skills. For example, learning to knit or crochet involves mastering new stitches and techniques, which can be both challenging and rewarding. Similarly, learning to sew or embroider involves developing an understanding of different types of fabric and thread and how to work with them effectively.

Crafting also provides an opportunity for self-expression. Whether making a quilt, a piece of jewellery or a painting, crafting allows individuals to express themselves in new and creative ways. Crafting can also provide a sense of relaxation and escape from everyday stressors, as it requires focus and concentration, which can help to calm the mind and reduce anxiety.

Another benefit of crafting is the opportunity to socialise with others who share similar interests. Many communities have craft groups or clubs that meet regularly, providing a sense of social connection and support. Crafting can also be a great way to connect with family members, as grandparents can teach grandchildren how to knit or sew, for example, creating a sense of intergenerational bonding.

Crafting is an excellent way to spend your retirement. It offers numerous physical and mental health benefits, the opportunity to learn new skills and express yourself creatively, and a sense of social connection and support. Whether you take up knitting, crocheting, sewing or another type of craft, the benefits are clear: crafting is a fun and fulfilling activity that can bring joy and happiness to your retirement years.

Here are some ideas for craft projects that retirees can explore:

- Knitting: Knitting is a relaxing and rewarding craft that can be enjoyed by people of all ages. Beginners can start with simple projects such as scarves, hats and dishcloths, while more experienced knitters can try their hand at sweaters, blankets and even socks.
- Crochet: Crochet is a versatile and portable craft that can be used to make everything from blankets and scarves to hats and toys. There are countless patterns available online, and crochet can be a great way to use up leftover yarn from other projects.
- Sewing: Sewing is a fun and practical craft that can be used to create clothing, home decor and accessories. Beginners can start with simple projects such as tote bags and cushions, while more experienced sewers

can try their hand at making dresses, jackets and quilts.
- Embroidery: Embroidery is a beautiful and versatile craft that can be used to embellish clothing, home decor and accessories. Beginners can start with simple stitches such as backstitch and satin stitch, while more experienced embroiderers can try more complex designs and techniques.
- Quilting: Quilting is a time-honoured craft that involves piecing together squares of fabric to create beautiful and functional quilts. There are countless quilt patterns available online, and quilting can be a great way to use up fabric scraps and create unique and personalised gifts.
- Jewellery making: Jewellery making is a fun and creative craft that can be used to create unique and personalised accessories. Beginners can start with simple beaded bracelets and earrings, while more experienced jewellers can try their hand at wire-wrapping and metalwork.
- Scrapbooking: Scrapbooking is a fun and creative way to preserve memories and create beautiful keepsakes. Beginners can start with simple layouts and designs, while more experienced scrapbookers can experiment with different techniques and materials.
- Painting: Painting is a relaxing and expressive craft that can be enjoyed by people of all skill levels. Beginners can start with simple watercolours or acrylics, while more experienced painters can experiment with oils and more complex techniques.
- Paper crafts: Paper crafting is a fun and versatile way to create unique and personalised cards, scrapbooks and other decorative items. Beginners can start with simple projects such as origami and paper flowers, while more experienced crafters can try their hand at card making and bookbinding.
- Woodworking: Woodworking is a rewarding and practical craft that can be used to make everything from furniture to decorative items. Beginners can start with simple projects such as birdhouses and picture frames, while more experienced woodworkers can try their hand at carving and cabinet making.
- Candle making: Candle making is a relaxing and aromatic craft that can be used to create beautiful and fragrant candles. Beginners can start with simple soy or beeswax candles, while more experienced candlemakers can experiment with different scents, colours and shapes.
- Soap Making: Soap making is a fun and creative craft that can be used to create unique and natural soaps. Beginners can start with simple melt-and-pour soap bases, while more experienced soap makers can experiment with different ingredients and scents.
- Mosaics: Mosaics are a beautiful and colourful way to create decorative items such as coasters, picture frames and mirrors. Beginners can start with simple mosaic kits, while more experienced mosaic artists can experiment with different materials such as glass and ceramics.
- Pottery: Pottery is a fun and tactile craft that involves shaping and

firing clay into beautiful and functional pieces. Beginners can start with simple handmade projects such as pinch pots and coil pots, while more experienced potters can experiment with throwing on a pottery wheel and glazing techniques.
- Cross-stitching: Cross-stitching is a relaxing and satisfying craft that creates colourful designs by stitching small X's onto fabric. Beginners can start with simple patterns such as bookmarks and small pictures, while more experienced cross stitchers can try more complex designs and techniques.
- Sculpture: Sculpture is a three-dimensional art form that can be created using a variety of materials such as clay, stone or metal. Beginners can start with simple projects such as modelling with clay or creating small sculptures with wire or papier-mâché, while more experienced sculptors can experiment with larger pieces and more complex techniques.
- Weaving: Weaving is a traditional craft involving the interlacing of threads or yarns to create fabrics or textiles. Beginners can start with simple projects such as weaving small mats or scarves, while more experienced weavers can experiment with different types of looms and complex weaving patterns.
- Macrame: Macrame is a knotting technique that can be used to create beautiful and intricate wall hangings, plant holders and jewellery. Beginners can start with simple projects such as key rings or bracelets, while more experienced macrame artists can experiment with more complex designs and techniques.
- Beading: Beading is a fun and creative way to create unique and personalised jewellery and accessories. Beginners can start with simple projects such as beaded bracelets or necklaces, while more experienced beaders can experiment with different types of beads and more complex designs.
- Leatherworking: Leatherworking is a versatile craft that can be used to make everything from wallets and belts to bags and shoes. Beginners can start with simple projects such as key rings or bookmarks, while more experienced leatherworkers can experiment with different types of leather and more complex techniques such as tooling and stamping.

Writing and Journaling for Personal Growth

Writing and journaling can be powerful tools for personal growth and self-discovery, especially for older people. These activities can help people reflect on their experiences, process their emotions and gain a deeper understanding of themselves and their lives.

Journaling is the practice of writing down one's thoughts, feelings and experiences in a notebook or journal. It is a private and personal practice that can be done anytime, anywhere. Writing, on the other hand, is a broader term that can encompass a variety of activities, including creative writing, memoir writing, and personal essay writing.

Writing and journaling can be particularly beneficial for retirees as it provides an opportunity to reflect on a lifetime of experiences, both positive and negative. Through the act of writing, retirees can gain a deeper understanding of themselves and their place in the world.

One of the benefits of writing and journaling is the opportunity to process and express emotions. Retirees may experience a range of emotions at this stage of life, including feelings of loss, regret or uncertainty about the future. By writing about these feelings, retirees can gain a deeper understanding of their emotions and find ways to deal with them in a healthy and constructive way.

Writing and journaling can also provide a sense of clarity and perspective. As retirees reflect on their lives and experiences, they may gain a new understanding of themselves and their values. Writing can help retirees articulate their beliefs and priorities and find meaning and purpose in their lives.

In addition to the emotional and psychological benefits, writing and journaling can also have physical benefits. Studies have shown that writing can improve immune system function, reduce stress and even lower blood pressure. Writing and journaling can also be a creative outlet, allowing retirees to express themselves in new and exciting ways.

Writing and journaling can be a way to connect with others and share experiences. Retirees may choose to share their writing with friends or family, or they may join a writing group or take a writing course. Sharing one's writing can be a way to find support and validation, and to connect with others who share similar interests and experiences.

Writing and journaling can be powerful tools for personal growth and self-discovery, especially for retirees. Through the act of writing, retirees can gain a deeper understanding of themselves and their lives, process their emotions, and find meaning and purpose in this stage of life. Whether it's journaling, creative writing or personal essays, writing can be a fulfilling and rewarding activity for retirees.

Pottery and Ceramics

Pottery and ceramics are traditional crafts that involve shaping clay into functional and decorative objects. These crafts have been practised for thousands of years and are still popular today, especially with retired people looking for a relaxing and creative activity.

Pottery and ceramics involve a variety of techniques including wheel throwing, hand building and glazing. Wheel throwing involves shaping clay on a potter's wheel, while hand building involves shaping clay by hand using a variety of techniques such as pinching, coiling and slab building. Glazing involves applying a layer of liquid glass to the surface of the clay object, which is then fired in a kiln to create a durable and waterproof finish.

Pottery and ceramics can be a rewarding and relaxing activity for retired people. It provides a sense of achievement in creating functional and beautiful objects that can be used or displayed in the home. Working with clay also has a meditative quality as it requires focus and concentration, which can help to reduce stress and anxiety. Can also be a social activity, as many communities have pottery studios or clubs where individuals can come together to work on their projects and share their skills and experiences. This can provide a sense of connection and camaraderie, as well as an opportunity to learn from others and improve your own skills.

Pottery and ceramics can also be a way to connect with nature and the environment. Working with clay involves using natural materials found in the earth, which can provide a sense of connection to the natural world. In addition, many potters and ceramic artists create objects that are inspired by nature, such as bowls and vases that resemble leaves or flowers.

Are traditional crafts that can provide a relaxing and creative activity for retirees. Whether one is working on the potter's wheel or hand-building clay, pottery and ceramics offer a sense of accomplishment, social connection, and creative expression. It can also provide a sense of connection to nature and the environment. Pottery and ceramics can be a rewarding and fulfilling activity for those in retirement, offering a way to explore their creativity and connect with others.

Here are some ideas for pottery and ceramics projects that retirees can explore:

• Functional pottery: Functional pottery, such as bowls, plates, and mugs, can be a fun and practical way to explore pottery and ceramics. Retirees can experiment with different shapes and sizes, and use glazes to create unique and personalized pieces that can be used in their homes.

• Sculptures: Pottery and ceramics can be used to create beautiful and unique sculptures. Retirees can experiment with different shapes and textures, and can use different techniques, such as carving and modeling, to create one-of-a-kind pieces.

• Garden ornaments: Pottery and ceramics can be used to create beautiful and durable garden ornaments, such as planters, bird baths, and stepping stones. Retirees can experiment with different shapes and sizes, and can use glazes and textures to create pieces that will withstand the elements.

• Tile making: Tile making is a fun and creative way to explore pottery and ceramics. Retirees can create unique and personalized tiles using a variety of techniques, such as stamping, painting, and glazing. These tiles can be used in home renovations or as decorative pieces.

• Clay jewelry: Pottery and ceramics can also be used to create beautiful and unique jewelry. Retirees can experiment with different shapes and sizes, and can use different techniques, such as carving and glazing, to create one-of-a-kind pieces that can be worn or given as gifts.

• Hand-built clay figures: Hand-building is a fun and creative way to explore pottery and ceramics. Retirees can experiment with different techniques, such as pinch pots and slab building, to create unique and personalized clay figures. These figures can be used as decorative pieces or as gifts for friends and family.

• Ceramic painting: Ceramic painting is a fun and creative way to explore pottery and ceramics. Retirees can use ceramic paints to create unique and personalized designs on pottery and ceramic pieces. These pieces can be used in their homes or given as gifts to friends and family.

Performing Arts

Performing arts is a form of artistic expression that involves the creation and presentation of a live performance to an audience. It can include a variety of art forms such as acting, singing, dancing and music performance. Participating in the performing arts can be an enjoyable and rewarding activity for retirees, providing opportunities for creative expression, socialising with others and promoting mental and physical health.

Acting is a form of performing arts that involves embodying a character and delivering scripted dialogue in front of an audience. Retirees can explore acting by joining a local theatre group or taking acting classes. This can be a great way to challenge yourself creatively and develop a new skill. Acting can also help improve communication skills and boost confidence.

Singing is another popular form of performing arts that retirees can enjoy. Singing can be a solo or group activity and can include a variety of genres such as pop, rock, jazz or classical music. Retirees can join a local choir or singing group, take private singing lessons, or participate in community musical theatre productions. Singing can be a fun and engaging way to express yourself creatively, while promoting mental and physical health.

Dancing is a form of performing arts that uses the body to express oneself creatively through movement. Retirees can explore different styles of dance, such as ballroom, swing or hip hop, by taking dance classes or joining a local dance group. Dancing can be a fun and engaging way to get exercise, socialise with others and express yourself creatively.

Music performance is another popular form of performing art that can be enjoyed by retirees. This can involve playing an instrument, such as the piano, guitar, or violin, or performing as part of a band or orchestra. Retirees can take private music lessons or join a local community band or orchestra. Music performance can provide a rewarding and engaging way to express oneself creatively, while also promoting mental and physical health.

The performing arts are a fun and engaging way for retirees to express themselves creatively, socialise with others and promote mental and physical health. Whether it's acting, singing, dancing or playing music, the performing arts offer a unique opportunity to explore new skills, challenge yourself creatively and connect with others in a fun and supportive environment.

- Acting in a local theater group: Join a local theater group and explore acting, character development, and stagecraft.
- Joining a community musical theater production: Participate in a musical theater production and explore singing, dancing, and acting.
- Learning to play a new instrument: Explore a new instrument and learn the techniques, styles, and music theory that accompany it.
- Performing in a one-person show: Create and perform a one-person show and explore writing, acting, and performance.
- Writing and performing a stand-up comedy routine: Write and perform a stand-up comedy routine and explore joke writing, delivery, and comedic timing.
- Learning a new dance style, such as salsa or tango: Learn a new dance style and explore the techniques, rhythms, and music theory that accompany it.
- Participating in a local dance competition: Participate in a local dance competition and explore choreography, technique, and performance.
- Creating and performing in a dance showcase: Create and perform in

a dance showcase and explore choreography, storytelling, and performance.
• Writing and performing a spoken-word piece: Write and perform a spoken-word piece and explore poetry, storytelling, and performance.
• Participating in a local poetry slam: Participate in a poetry slam and explore poetry, performance, and audience engagement.
• Performing in a storytelling event: Perform in a storytelling event and explore storytelling, performance, and audience engagement.
• Learning to juggle or perform magic tricks: Learn to juggle or perform magic tricks and explore dexterity, coordination, and performance.
• Creating and performing a puppet show: Create and perform a puppet show and explore puppetry, storytelling, and performance.
• Participating in a local circus or acrobatics class: Participate in a circus or acrobatics class and explore acrobatics, performance, and storytelling.
• Joining a local drum circle: Join a local drum circle and explore percussion, rhythm, and performance.
• Performing in a local street performance festival: Participate in a local street performance festival and explore performance, audience engagement, and storytelling.
• Participating in a local Renaissance festival: Participate in a local Renaissance festival and explore performance, costume design, and storytelling.

Homebrewing

Homebrewing is a popular hobby among retirees who enjoy experimenting with different flavours and styles of beer or cider. It can also be a social activity, as homebrewers often get together to share their creations and exchange brewing tips and techniques.

To get started with homebrewing, retirees will need some basic equipment, including a brew kettle, fermenter and bottling equipment. Online classes and tutorials are available to help beginners learn the basics of brewing, including equipment, ingredients and technique. With practice and experimentation, retirees can create their own unique brews to share with friends and family.

One of the benefits of homebrewing is the ability to control the ingredients and flavours in the beer or cider. Homebrewers can choose from a wide variety of grains, hops and yeasts to create different styles of beer or cider. They can also experiment with different flavours, such as fruit or spices, to create unique and delicious brews.

Homebrewing can also be a cost-effective alternative to buying beer or cider in a shop. While there is an upfront investment in equipment, the cost of ingredients is usually less than buying beer or cider in a shop. And the satisfaction of creating something with your own hands can be a fulfilling and rewarding experience.

As well as creating delicious beers, homebrewing can provide retirees with a sense of community and social engagement. There are many homebrewing clubs and events across the country where homebrewers can get together to share their creations and exchange brewing tips and techniques. These clubs and events can be a great way for retirees to meet new people and make new friends with similar interests.

Overall, homebrewing can be a fun and fulfilling hobby for retirees who enjoy experimenting with different flavours and styles of beer or cider. With so many resources available online and in person, retirees can continue to learn and develop their homebrewing skills throughout retirement.

HOBBIES AND INTERESTS

Retirement is a fantastic opportunity to explore new hobbies and interests or dive deeper into existing ones. With the gift of time, retirees can truly immerse themselves in activities they've always been passionate about or even discover new passions. This article provides an overview of four creative hobbies to consider when planning for an enriching retirement.

Picking Up a New Instrument

Music has a magical ability to bring joy, relaxation, and mental stimulation to our lives. Learning to play a new instrument during retirement can be an immensely rewarding experience. Whether you've always dreamt of strumming the guitar or mastering the piano, retirement is the perfect time to start. Playing an instrument not only helps keep your mind sharp but also provides opportunities to connect with others, either through group lessons or jam sessions with fellow musicians.

When considering picking up a new instrument during retirement, it's important to choose one that aligns with your interests, physical abilities, and lifestyle. Here are some ideas to help you get started:

- Ukulele: The ukulele is a small, portable, and relatively easy-to-learn instrument. Its soft, cheerful sound makes it a popular choice for retirees looking to start playing music.
- Keyboard/Piano: Learning to play the keyboard or piano provides a solid foundation in music theory and can lead to playing a variety of music styles. Digital keyboards offer a more portable and budget-friendly option compared to traditional pianos.
- Acoustic Guitar: The acoustic guitar is versatile and great for playing various music genres. With its soothing tones and wide range of available learning resources, it's an ideal choice for retirees.
- Harmonica: Compact, affordable, and easy to learn, the harmonica is perfect for those looking to make music on the go. It's suitable for playing blues, folk, and even classical tunes.
- Recorder: This simple woodwind instrument is often taught in schools and is an excellent introduction to playing music. It's inexpensive, easy to learn, and can be played solo or in ensembles.
- Percussion: Learning percussion instruments such as the djembe, cajon, or bongos can be an engaging and therapeutic way to express yourself through rhythm.
- Community Bands or Orchestras: If you have prior experience playing

an instrument or are interested in learning one like the violin, flute, or trumpet, consider joining a community band or orchestra. This offers a more structured and social environment for learning and playing music.

- Electronic Wind Instruments (EWI): These instruments simulate the sound of various wind instruments using digital technology. They're portable, versatile, and great for those with limited space or physical constraints.
- Autoharp: An easy-to-learn stringed instrument, the autoharp is perfect for retirees looking to accompany themselves while singing or play simple melodies.
- Mandolin: A small, stringed instrument with a distinctive sound, the mandolin is great for playing folk, bluegrass, and classical music.
- Handpan: A unique percussion instrument, the handpan produces soothing, ethereal melodies and is excellent for relaxation and stress relief.
- Dulcimer: The dulcimer is a stringed instrument played on the lap, making it an accessible option for retirees with mobility issues. It's particularly suited to playing folk music.
- Kalimba: Also known as a thumb piano, the kalimba is a compact, handheld instrument that produces a melodic, calming sound. It's easy to learn and transport, making it perfect for retirees.
- Accordion: A versatile instrument used in many music styles, the accordion offers a fun and engaging challenge for retirees looking to explore their musical abilities.
- Cello: For those interested in classical music, the cello offers a rich, deep sound and a rewarding learning experience.
- Banjo: The banjo is a popular choice for playing bluegrass, country, and folk music. It's a unique instrument that can be enjoyed as a solo player or in a group setting.
- Ocarina: This small, flute-like instrument is easy to learn, portable, and produces a sweet, melodic sound. It's an ideal option for retirees looking to explore wind instruments.

Painting, Drawing, and Sculpting

Retirement is the perfect time to explore your creative side through painting, drawing and sculpting. These artistic pursuits offer endless opportunities for self-expression and personal growth, regardless of your skill level or previous experience. Engaging in these activities can help you relax, reduce stress and even improve cognitive function as you challenge yourself to learn new techniques and styles.

Painting allows you to experiment with a variety of media, such as watercolours, acrylics or oils, each offering unique characteristics and textures. You can choose to paint landscapes, portraits or abstract compositions, depending on your interests and artistic goals. Painting can also be a wonderful way to connect with nature by working outdoors, known as plein air painting, where you can capture the beauty of your surroundings first hand.

Drawing is a versatile art form that can be done with a variety of materials including graphite, charcoal, coloured pencils or even digital tools such as tablets and pens. Drawing is an excellent way to develop your powers of observation and hone your artistic skills. Whether you're sketching a still life, creating detailed illustrations or designing whimsical characters, the world of drawing offers countless opportunities to express your creativity.

Sculpting is a three-dimensional art form that allows you to bring your imagination to life through the manipulation of materials such as clay, wood or metal. Working with your hands to shape and form sculptures can be incredibly rewarding and therapeutic, providing a tangible connection to your artistic creations. Sculpture also offers a unique challenge in that it requires you to consider elements such as balance, proportion and structure in your work.

To get started with painting, drawing or sculpting, consider taking local art classes, watching online tutorials or investing in instructional books. Art classes can provide valuable guidance and feedback from experienced teachers, as well as the opportunity to meet other like-minded people who share your passion for art. As you progress in your artistic journey, you may wish to create a dedicated workspace in your home, complete with the necessary tools, materials and inspiration to fuel your creativity.

Ultimately, painting, drawing and sculpting in retirement can lead to a more fulfilling and enriching life. Embrace your inner artist and enjoy the process of learning, experimenting and creating as you discover the joys of these timeless art forms.

Photography: Capturing Life's Beauty

Photography is a captivating hobby that allows you to capture the beauty of life and the world around you in striking visual images. Retirement is the ideal time to delve deeper into this artistic pursuit, as you'll have ample opportunity to explore different aspects of photography and hone your skills. Whether you're interested in landscape, portrait, wildlife or street photography, the possibilities are endless when it comes to preserving memories and moments through the art of photography.

Investing in a quality camera and learning the basics of composition, lighting and editing can greatly enhance the images you produce. Beginners may want to start with an easy-to-use digital camera before moving on to more advanced equipment, such as a digital single lens reflex (DSLR) or mirrorless camera, which offer more control over settings and produce higher quality images.

As well as mastering your equipment, it's important to develop your photographer's eye. This means learning to see the world around you with a heightened sense of observation and awareness, noticing details, patterns and beauty in everyday life. It's this unique perspective that will enable you to create truly stunning photographs that tell a story or evoke emotion in the viewer.

One of the most enjoyable aspects of photography is the opportunity to explore new places and experiences. Whether you're travelling to exotic destinations, hiking through nature reserves or simply wandering the streets of your hometown, photography can serve as a source of inspiration and adventure during your retirement years.

As your photography journey progresses, consider attending workshops, courses or joining a local photography club. These communities offer valuable support, feedback and camaraderie among fellow enthusiasts. Sharing your work with others, either in person or online, can be a rewarding way to receive constructive criticism, learn new techniques and grow as a photographer.

Photography also offers the opportunity to express your unique artistic vision through the use of editing software such as Adobe Lightroom or Photoshop. By enhancing colours, adjusting exposure and applying creative effects, you can transform your images into captivating works of art that truly reflect your personal style.

Photography is a deeply rewarding hobby that allows you to capture the beauty of life and create lasting visual memories throughout your retirement years. By investing time in learning the craft, developing your artistic vision and exploring the world around you, you can create a fulfilling and enriching pastime that brings joy and inspiration to both you and those who view your work.

Joining a Book Club

Joining a book club in retirement can be an enjoyable way to engage with literature while fostering connections with fellow book lovers. Book clubs provide an intellectually stimulating environment where you can delve into a wide range of genres and discover new authors and perspectives. By participating in lively discussions, you can not only broaden your literary horizons, but also deepen your understanding of the world and the human experience.

One of the main benefits of a book club is the opportunity for social interaction. Retirement can sometimes lead to feelings of isolation or loneliness, but book clubs bring people together through a shared passion for reading. Engaging in thoughtful conversation with like-minded people can lead to lasting friendships and a strong sense of belonging to a community.

Book clubs also encourage you to read more frequently and consistently, as they provide a structure and schedule for exploring new books. By setting aside time to read and discuss books with others, you can create a routine that fosters personal growth and intellectual curiosity in your retirement years. This habit can help keep your mind sharp and promote mental well-being.

To find a book club that fits your interests and schedule, you can explore several options, including local libraries, community centres, or online platforms. Many libraries and community centres offer book clubs that cater to different tastes, from classic literature to contemporary fiction or non-fiction. Online book clubs, accessible through websites or social media groups, offer a convenient and flexible option for those who prefer to participate from the comfort of their own home.

If you can't find a book club that suits your tastes, consider starting your own. By gathering a group of friends or acquaintances who share your enthusiasm for reading, you can create a book club experience tailored to your specific interests and literary tastes.

In addition to fostering a love of reading, book clubs can also inspire other activities and hobbies. For example, some book clubs include themed meals, movie nights, or guest speakers related to the books being read. These activities can add an extra layer of enjoyment and enrichment to your book club experience.

Joining a book club in retirement can provide many benefits, including intellectual stimulation, social connection and personal growth. By immersing yourself in the world of literature and engaging in meaningful discussions with other book lovers, you can create a fulfilling and enriching pastime that will enhance your retirement years.

SPORTS AND FITNESS

Retirement is an excellent time to prioritize your health and well-being through sports and fitness activities. Staying active not only benefits your physical health but also improves your mental and emotional well-being. This article outlines nine different sports and fitness activities that cater to various interests and fitness levels, providing retirees with a wealth of options for staying active and engaged.

Swimming for Health and Relaxation

Swimming is a wonderful activity for retired people to maintain their health and wellbeing while enjoying relaxation. As a low-impact exercise, swimming is easy on the joints, making it an excellent choice for people with arthritis or other joint problems. The buoyancy of the water supports the body, reducing stress on muscles and bones and allowing a greater range of motion.

In addition to the physical benefits, swimming is an effective cardiovascular workout, helping to improve heart health, lung function and circulation. Regular swimming sessions can help maintain or even increase endurance, muscle strength and overall fitness levels. The resistance provided by the water during swimming also helps to tone and strengthen muscles, contributing to a leaner and more robust physique.

Swimming also has mental health benefits. The rhythmic nature of the strokes, combined with the calming effect of being immersed in water, can induce a meditative state that helps to reduce stress and promote relaxation. Swimming can also stimulate the release of endorphins, the body's natural feel-good chemicals, which can improve mood and help combat anxiety and depression.

Retirees can engage in different types of swimming activities to suit their preferences and fitness levels. For those seeking a more structured swimming programme, many community pools and fitness centres offer adult swimming lessons, water aerobics classes or lap swimming sessions. These organised activities provide guidance, motivation and a sense of camaraderie with fellow swimmers.

For those who prefer a more leisurely approach, swimming at a local beach, lake or outdoor pool can be a refreshing and enjoyable way to stay active while enjoying the benefits of nature and fresh air.

Regardless of your swimming environment or goals, it's essential to practice water safety and be aware of your limits. Investing in appropriate swimwear, goggles, and other accessories can enhance your swimming experience and ensure you remain comfortable and safe in the water.

Golf: A Social and Competitive Sport

Golf is often seen as both a social and a competitive sport, so it is not surprising that many people turn to it in retirement, when they have more free time and the desire to stay active in their golden years. As a sport, golf offers many opportunities for retirees to get some exercise, make new friends and challenge themselves mentally and physically.

As people enter their retirement years, staying active becomes increasingly important for maintaining overall health and well-being. Golf is an excellent low-impact sport that allows retirees to stay fit without putting too much stress on their bodies. With its emphasis on running, swinging and coordination, golf can help retirees improve their cardiovascular health, strength and flexibility.

In addition to its physical benefits, golf offers a wealth of social opportunities. Many retirees have more time on their hands, and golf provides a natural environment for making new friends and connections. Whether it's joining a local golf club or simply chatting with fellow golfers on the course, golf fosters camaraderie and a sense of belonging.

The competitive aspect of golf can also appeal to retirees as a way to challenge themselves and stay mentally sharp. Golf is a game of skill and strategy, and many retirees appreciate the opportunity to hone their skills and compete against others. Golf tournaments and friendly matches among peers can add an element of excitement and motivation to the sport, keeping retirees engaged and eager to continue playing.

Golf also offers retirees the opportunity to travel and explore new courses around the world. With countless golf destinations and resorts available, many retirees choose to incorporate golf into their holiday plans. This not only broadens their golfing horizons, but also allows them to experience new cultures and sights along the way.

Golf is a sport that offers retirees the perfect blend of social interaction, physical activity and mental stimulation. As they move into their golden years, many people find that golf helps them stay active, make new friends and maintain a competitive spirit. With its unique combination of benefits, golf continues to be a popular choice for retirees looking to enrich their lives and enjoy their well-earned leisure time.

Yoga and Meditation for Mind and Body Wellness

Yoga and meditation have long been recognised for their many benefits in promoting physical and mental wellbeing. As individuals enter retirement, incorporating these practices into their daily routines can provide a wealth of benefits for overall health and well-being. With more time and flexibility in their schedules, retirees can take full advantage of the transformative effects of yoga and meditation, allowing them to nurture their mental, emotional and physical health during this important stage of life.

One of the most significant benefits of yoga is its ability to improve physical health, especially for retirees who may be experiencing age-related changes in their bodies. Through a series of postures and stretches, yoga helps to improve flexibility, balance and strength. These improvements can in turn help alleviate common age-related problems such as joint pain, muscle stiffness and reduced mobility. In addition, yoga can contribute to cardiovascular health by promoting good circulation and helping to regulate blood pressure.

Beyond the physical benefits, yoga also offers retirees the opportunity to cultivate mental and emotional well-being. As a mind-body practice, yoga promotes mindfulness and self-awareness, allowing practitioners to become more in tune with their thoughts and emotions. By fostering this connection, retirees can develop healthier coping mechanisms for managing stress, anxiety and other emotional challenges that may arise during their golden years.

Meditation, often practised in conjunction with yoga, is another powerful tool for promoting wellbeing in retirement. This ancient practice involves focusing the mind and cultivating awareness, helping individuals to develop a greater sense of inner peace and tranquillity. Regular meditation practice can have numerous positive effects on mental health, including reduced stress, improved emotional regulation and enhanced cognitive function. These benefits can be particularly valuable to retirees as they navigate the emotional and psychological changes that often accompany this stage of life.

In addition, both yoga and meditation can provide retirees with opportunities for social engagement and community involvement. Many local yoga studios and community centres offer classes specifically designed for older adults, creating a supportive and welcoming environment for retirees to connect with like-minded individuals. These connections can help foster a sense of belonging and contribute to overall happiness and well-being.

Yoga and meditation offer retirees a holistic approach to mind and body wellness that can significantly improve their quality of life. By adopting these practices, retirees can cultivate greater physical health, mental clarity and emotional resilience, helping them to face the challenges and opportunities of retirement with grace and ease. In addition, the social connections made through yoga and meditation can further contribute to overall well-being, making these practices a valuable addition to any retiree's daily routine.

Cycling Adventures

Cycling is an activity that has long been celebrated for its many health and leisure benefits, making it an ideal pursuit for those entering their retirement years. With more time and flexibility, retirees can embark on exciting cycling adventures that allow them to stay active, explore new environments and cultivate a sense of personal achievement. As they navigate this stage of life, many retirees find that cycling offers unique opportunities to broaden their horizons and create lasting memories.

One of the most attractive aspects of cycling for retirees is its versatility as a form of exercise. Cycling can be tailored to an individual's fitness level and preferences, allowing retirees to choose between leisurely rides on flat terrain or more challenging routes with hills and inclines. This adaptability ensures that cycling remains an enjoyable and accessible activity for people of all ages and abilities, promoting cardiovascular health, muscle strength and overall physical fitness.

As retirees embark on their cycling adventures, they may choose to explore local trails and routes within their own communities. This can give them a fresh perspective on their surroundings and a deeper appreciation for the natural beauty and hidden gems that are right on their doorstep. In addition, cycling can provide retirees with a sense of accomplishment and satisfaction as they conquer new trails and set personal goals for distance, speed or endurance.

For those looking to venture further afield, cycling holidays and tours are an increasingly popular option for retirees seeking unique travel experiences. Companies specialising in cycling holidays often offer a range of options to suit different fitness levels, interests and destinations. From guided group tours through scenic landscapes to self-guided expeditions along historic routes, there is no shortage of opportunities for retirees to discover new places and cultures from the vantage point of a bicycle seat.

In addition to the sense of adventure that cycling provides, it also offers many opportunities for social contact and camaraderie. Many retirees choose to join cycling clubs or take part in group rides, where they can make new friends with other cycling enthusiasts. These social interactions can contribute to a sense of belonging and purpose, helping to combat the feelings of loneliness and isolation that can sometimes accompany retirement.

Cycling in retirement can be an excellent opportunity for personal growth and self-discovery. As retirees tackle new challenges and overcome obstacles on their cycling journeys, they often find that they develop greater confidence, resilience and independence. These personal qualities can carry over into other aspects of their lives, enabling retirees to approach their golden years with optimism and enthusiasm.

Cycling adventures can range from leisurely rides through picturesque landscapes to challenging expeditions across diverse terrains. Here are some ideas for cycling adventures that cater to different interests and skill levels:

- Wine Country Tours: Explore renowned wine regions like Napa Valley, California, or Bordeaux, France, on a bike. Cycle between vineyards, enjoy wine tastings, and learn about the art of winemaking.
- Coastal Rides: Cycle along stunning coastlines, such as the Pacific Coast Highway in California, the Amalfi Coast in Italy, or the Great Ocean Road in Australia. Enjoy breathtaking views, charming seaside towns, and fresh sea air.
- Historic Routes: Travel through history by cycling along ancient trade routes like the Silk Road in Central Asia, the Camino de Santiago in Spain, or the Via Francigena from Canterbury, England, to Rome, Italy.
- Mountain Challenges: Test your endurance by cycling through mountain ranges such as the Rockies in North America, the Alps in Europe, or the Andes in South America. Conquer challenging climbs, enjoy exhilarating descents, and take in spectacular vistas.
- National Park Tours: Discover the natural beauty of national parks like Yellowstone and Grand Teton in the United States, Banff and Jasper in Canada, or Fiordland in New Zealand. Cycle through diverse landscapes, encounter wildlife, and learn about the unique ecosystems.
- Island Hopping: Explore beautiful archipelagos like the Greek Islands, the Canary Islands, or the Hawaiian Islands by bike. Cycle from one island to another using ferries, and experience the distinct culture, landscapes, and cuisine of each island.

- Rail Trails: Enjoy leisurely rides along converted railway lines, such as the Katy Trail in Missouri, the Otago Central Rail Trail in New Zealand, or the Danube Cycle Path in Europe. These trails often feature gentle gradients, making them suitable for cyclists of all levels.
- Urban Exploration: Discover the charm of iconic cities like Amsterdam, Copenhagen, or Tokyo on two wheels. Cycle through historic neighborhoods, visit famous landmarks, and enjoy local cuisine.
- Charity Rides: Participate in organized charity rides like the Ride to Conquer Cancer, the MS Bike Tour, or the AIDS/LifeCycle. Raise funds for a worthy cause while enjoying the camaraderie of fellow cyclists and the sense of accomplishment from completing a challenging ride.
- Customized Cycling Adventures: Plan your own unique cycling adventure based on your interests, fitness level, and desired destinations. Create an itinerary that combines cycling with other activities like hiking, kayaking, or cultural experiences.

Low-Impact Sports and Games

Low-impact sports and games are an ideal choice for retirees looking to maintain an active lifestyle while minimizing the risk of injury or strain on their bodies. Activities such as bocce ball, lawn bowling, or pickleball offer an enjoyable and social way for older adults to stay engaged, both physically and mentally, as they navigate their retirement years.

- Bocce ball, an ancient Italian game, involves tossing or rolling balls towards a smaller target ball, known as the "pallino." This game can be played on grass, sand, or specialized courts, making it a versatile and accessible option for retirees. Bocce encourages precision and strategy while also allowing for social interaction and friendly competition.
- Lawn bowling, similar to bocce, requires players to roll slightly asymmetrical balls towards a smaller target ball, called the "jack." Played on a flat, manicured grass surface, lawn bowling combines skill, strategy, and a moderate level of physical activity. Many lawn bowling clubs cater specifically to older adults, providing an excellent opportunity for retirees to connect with like-minded individuals.
- Pickleball, a relatively recent addition to the world of low-impact sports, combines elements of tennis, badminton, and table tennis. Played on a smaller court with a lightweight paddle and a plastic ball, pickleball is easy on the joints and accessible to players of varying skill levels. The sport's growing popularity has led to the establishment of pickleball clubs and community leagues, making it easy for retirees to find playing partners and participate in organized events.
- Beyond the physical benefits, engaging in low-impact sports and games can have a significant positive impact on the mental and emotional

well-being of retirees. These activities provide opportunities for social connection, helping to combat feelings of loneliness and isolation that can sometimes accompany retirement. Furthermore, participating in friendly competition can contribute to a sense of purpose and accomplishment, promoting overall happiness and life satisfaction.

- Low-impact sports and games, such as bocce ball, lawn bowling, or pickleball, offer retirees an enjoyable way to stay active and engaged during their golden years. These activities promote physical health, social interaction, and mental well-being, making them a valuable addition to any retiree's lifestyle. By exploring these low-impact sports and games, retirees can enhance their quality of life and make the most of their leisure time.

Tai Chi and Qigong for Balance and Flexibility

Tai Chi and Qigong are time-honoured Chinese practices that have gained popularity around the world for their many health benefits, particularly for older adults. As retirees seek gentle yet effective ways to maintain their physical and mental well-being, tai chi and qigong offer ideal options for improving balance, flexibility and overall well-being in a mindful and meditative way.

Often referred to as "meditation in motion", Tai Chi is a low-impact martial art that emphasises slow, graceful movements synchronised with deep, focused breathing. By concentrating on the precise execution of each movement, practitioners develop greater body awareness and mindfulness. For retirees, tai chi offers a wealth of benefits, including improved balance and coordination, which can be particularly valuable in preventing falls and maintaining independence.

Qigong, closely related to Tai Chi, is another ancient Chinese practice that combines slow, flowing movements with deep, rhythmic breathing and mental focus. Qigong exercises are designed to cultivate and balance the body's vital energy, or 'qi', and promote overall health and well-being. For retirees, Qigong offers many benefits, including increased flexibility, improved circulation and reduced stress.

Both tai chi and qigong are accessible to people of all ages and fitness levels, making them particularly suitable for retirees looking for low-impact exercise options. These practices can be easily adapted to accommodate physical limitations or health concerns, ensuring that participants can enjoy the benefits of these disciplines without the risk of injury or strain.

In addition to their physical benefits, Tai Chi and Qigong can also contribute to the mental and emotional well-being of retirees. The meditative aspects of these practices encourage mindfulness, relaxation, and stress reduction, helping individuals to cultivate a greater sense of inner peace and tranquility. As retirees navigate the emotional and psychological shifts that often accompany this stage of life, Tai Chi and Qigong can provide valuable tools for maintaining emotional balance and resilience.

Furthermore, Tai Chi and Qigong classes often foster a sense of community and social connection, as participants gather to practice and learn together. Retirees can benefit from the camaraderie and support of fellow practitioners, helping to combat feelings of loneliness or isolation that can sometimes arise during retirement.

Tai Chi and Qigong present retirees with gentle, meditative ways to enhance their balance, flexibility, and overall well-being. By incorporating these ancient Chinese practices into their routines, retirees can enjoy the numerous physical, mental, and emotional benefits that these disciplines have to offer. With their focus on slow, deliberate movements, deep breathing, and mental concentration, Tai Chi and Qigong provide ideal opportunities for retirees to cultivate holistic wellness and thrive during their golden years.

Exploring Alternative Therapies and Treatments

Exploring alternative therapies and treatments can be a valuable approach to maintaining and enhancing overall health, particularly for retirees who may be experiencing age-related changes in their bodies. As people navigate their retirement years, integrating alternative therapies such as acupuncture, massage, or chiropractic care into their wellness routines can provide a holistic and complementary approach to addressing issues like pain management, stress relief, and overall well-being.

Acupuncture, a traditional Chinese medicine practice, involves the insertion of fine needles at specific points on the body to stimulate and balance the flow of vital energy or "qi." This ancient technique has been used to address a wide range of conditions, including chronic pain, headaches, and anxiety. For retirees, acupuncture can offer a non-invasive, drug-free approach to managing age-related aches and pains or coping with stress and emotional challenges.

Massage therapy, another popular alternative treatment, involves the manipulation of soft tissues, such as muscles and connective tissue, to promote relaxation and alleviate discomfort. Regular massages can help retirees manage chronic pain, reduce muscle tension, and improve circulation, which can be particularly beneficial for those experiencing age-related stiffness or mobility issues. Furthermore, massage therapy can contribute to stress relief and promote a greater sense of well-being.

Chiropractic care, which focuses on the alignment and function of the spine and musculoskeletal system, can also offer retirees numerous benefits. Chiropractic adjustments can help to alleviate joint pain, improve range of motion, and enhance overall mobility. By addressing spinal misalignments and promoting optimal nervous system function, chiropractic care can contribute to improved overall health and wellness for retirees.

In addition to these therapies, retirees may explore other alternative treatments, such as herbal medicine, aromatherapy, or reiki, to further support their well-being. These treatments can provide a more holistic approach to health, addressing the interconnectedness of the mind, body, and spirit.

Before embarking on any alternative therapy or treatment, it is important for retirees to consult with their healthcare providers to ensure that these practices are suitable and safe for their individual needs and circumstances. By working closely with their healthcare team, retirees can develop a personalized wellness plan that integrates alternative therapies with conventional medical care.

In summary, alternative therapies and treatments, such as acupuncture, massage, and chiropractic care, can provide retirees with valuable tools for managing pain, reducing stress, and enhancing overall wellness. By exploring these complementary approaches to health, retirees can support their physical, mental, and emotional well-being in a holistic manner, allowing them to fully embrace the opportunities and challenges that retirement brings.

Water Aerobics and Aquatic Exercises

Water aerobics and aquatic exercises are becoming increasingly popular as low-impact fitness options, offering numerous health benefits while minimizing the risk of injury. These types of activities are particularly well-suited for retirees, especially those with joint issues or mobility challenges, as the buoyancy of water provides support for the body and reduces stress on the joints.

Water aerobics classes, which typically take place in shallow pools, involve a variety of exercises set to music and led by a certified instructor. The classes incorporate movements such as marching, jogging, kicking, and jumping jacks, as well as the use of equipment like foam noodles and water dumbbells. The water's resistance provides a natural form of strength training, while the rhythmic movements elevate the heart rate, promoting cardiovascular fitness.

Aquatic exercises, which may be performed individually or as part of a group, encompass a wide range of activities that can be tailored to individual fitness levels and goals. These exercises may include swimming laps, water walking or jogging, resistance training with pool equipment, or flexibility and balance exercises using the support of the pool's edge or a flotation device.

The buoyancy of water provides numerous benefits for retirees engaging in water aerobics and aquatic exercises. By partially supporting the body's weight, the water reduces the impact on joints, making these activities ideal for individuals with arthritis, osteoporosis, or other joint-related issues. This buoyancy also allows for a greater range of motion, which can help improve flexibility and functional movement.

In addition to their physical benefits, water aerobics and aquatic exercises offer several advantages for the mental and emotional well-being of retirees. The social aspect of group classes can help combat feelings of isolation or loneliness that sometimes accompany retirement, while the soothing properties of water can contribute to stress relief and relaxation.

Furthermore, the supportive environment of water-based activities can be particularly beneficial for retirees who may be dealing with age-related changes in balance or mobility. The water's buoyancy can help prevent falls and provide a sense of security, allowing participants to build confidence and maintain independence in their fitness routines.

Water aerobics and aquatic exercises offer retirees an excellent low-impact fitness option that combines cardiovascular and strength training benefits with the unique advantages of exercising in water. By supporting the body and reducing stress on joints, these activities are particularly suitable for individuals with joint issues or mobility challenges. By participating in water-based fitness activities, retirees can enjoy improved physical health, social connection, and mental well-being, helping them to thrive during their golden years.

TECHNOLOGY AND ENTERTAINMENT

Technology and entertainment have become increasingly intertwined over the years, revolutionising the way we consume and engage with different forms of media. As you navigate your retirement years, embracing the intersection of technology and entertainment can greatly enhance your leisure time, offering a wealth of options for personal enrichment, relaxation and connection with others.

One of the most significant impacts of technology on entertainment has been the rise of on-demand content platforms, such as streaming services for movies, TV shows, music and podcasts. These platforms give you the freedom to access a vast library of content whenever and wherever you want, allowing you to tailor your entertainment experience to your individual interests and preferences. With the convenience of technology at your fingertips, you can explore new genres, artists and creators at your own pace and on your own terms.

In addition, technology has changed the way we engage with entertainment, providing opportunities for interactivity and personalisation. Video games, for example, offer immersive experiences that go beyond passive consumption, allowing you to actively participate in exciting narratives and challenges. Similarly, social media platforms allow you to connect with creators and fellow enthusiasts, fostering communities and discussions around shared interests.

Another notable development in technology and entertainment is the increasing availability of accessible and user-friendly devices and platforms. From smart TVs and voice-activated speakers to tablets and e-readers, there are many devices designed to simplify and streamline your entertainment experience. These devices often include built-in accessibility features such as adjustable font sizes, voice control and subtitles, making it easier for people of all ages and abilities to enjoy the full range of entertainment options.

Technology has also enabled new forms of artistic expression and creativity, such as digital photography, filmmaking and graphic design. By embracing these digital tools and platforms, you can pursue your passions and develop new skills in retirement, cultivating a deeper connection with the world of entertainment and self-expression.

As you explore the evolving landscape of technology and entertainment, it's important to remain open and adaptable. Change can be challenging, but embracing new tools and platforms can lead to rewarding experiences and discoveries. By keeping abreast of the latest developments and seeking out resources to support your learning journey, you can unlock the full potential of technology to enrich your retirement years.

The integration of technology and entertainment offers a wealth of opportunities for personal growth, connection and enjoyment in retirement. By exploring the different types of media, devices and platforms available, you can create a personalised and engaging entertainment experience that meets your individual needs and desires, ultimately enhancing your overall quality of life.

Embracing New Technologies and Gadgets

Embracing new technologies and gadgets in retirement can be an enriching and empowering experience that can greatly enhance your quality of life. As you embark on this exciting new chapter, keeping up to date with the latest technological advances can help you maintain a sense of independence, explore new hobbies and stay connected with friends and family.

One of the biggest benefits of familiarising yourself with new technologies is the ability to stay in touch with loved ones. With the rise of social media platforms and communication apps, it has never been easier to keep up with the lives of your children, grandchildren and friends. By using these digital tools, you can share photos, make video calls and participate in group chats, ensuring you stay connected and involved in the lives of those who matter most.

Beyond communication, new technologies can also help you explore and develop new hobbies and interests. From digital photography and video editing to learning a new language or mastering a musical instrument, there are countless apps and devices available to support your personal growth and development. By keeping an open mind and actively seeking out new experiences, you can continue to learn and grow throughout your retirement years.

Another important aspect of embracing new technology is staying informed about the latest devices and platforms designed specifically for older adults. These user-friendly tools often have larger displays, simplified interfaces and built-in accessibility options to ensure they are both easy to use and easy on the eyes. Researching and investing in these specialised devices can greatly improve your overall experience and help you feel more confident in your ability to navigate the digital world.

As you begin your journey into the world of new technologies and gadgets, it's important to approach the learning process with patience and persistence. You may encounter challenges and frustrations along the way, but remember that mastering new skills takes time and practice. Don't be afraid to seek out resources such as tutorials, workshops or even tech-savvy friends and family members to guide and support you as you learn.

Embracing new technologies and gadgets in retirement can be a fulfilling and rewarding experience that opens up a world of possibilities. By keeping an open mind and actively seeking out new tools and platforms, you can continue to grow, connect and thrive in today's increasingly digital landscape. Whether it's exploring new hobbies, staying in touch with loved ones or simply enjoying the convenience of modern technology, the benefits of embracing this brave new world are truly limitless.

As you explore the world of new technologies and gadgets, consider the following ideas that can enhance various aspects of your life in retirement:

• Smart home devices: Devices such as Amazon Echo and Google Home can simplify your daily life by letting you control your home's lighting, temperature and security using just your voice. They can also provide information, play music and set reminders.

• Wearable fitness trackers: Devices such as Fitbit and Apple Watch can help you monitor your physical activity, heart rate and sleep patterns, encouraging you to maintain a healthy lifestyle in retirement.

• Digital assistants for seniors: Specialised devices such as the GrandPad and Jitterbug Smart2 offer simplified interfaces and features tailored for older adults, making it easier to stay in touch with loved ones, browse the web and access various apps.

• E-readers: Devices such as the Kindle and Nook allow you to carry an entire library of books in a lightweight, portable device. Adjustable font sizes and backlight options make for a more comfortable reading experience.

• Virtual reality headsets: Gadgets like Oculus Quest and PlayStation VR offer immersive experiences in gaming, travel and education, transporting you to new worlds and environments.

• Smart home security systems: Advanced security systems like Ring and Nest provide peace of mind with features like video doorbells, smart locks, and remote monitoring to keep your home safe.

• Telehealth devices: Devices such as TytoCare and KardiaMobile allow you to monitor your health and consult with healthcare professionals remotely, making healthcare more accessible and convenient.

• Robotic vacuum cleaners: Devices such as Roomba and Roborock can automate your cleaning tasks, helping you maintain a tidy home with minimal effort.

• Smart thermostats: Devices like Nest and Ecobee can automatically adjust your home's temperature based on your preferences and habits, improving energy efficiency and comfort.

• Language Learning Apps and Devices: Tools like Duolingo and Rosetta Stone can help you learn new languages through interactive lessons and exercises, broadening your cultural horizons and keeping your mind sharp.

Exploring Virtual Reality and Video Games

Exploring the world of virtual reality and video games in retirement can be an engaging and stimulating experience. As you enter this new phase of life, it's important to stay cognitively active and socially connected, and immersing yourself in the world of gaming can help you achieve both of these goals. Virtual reality, in particular, offers an immersive experience that transports you to different environments and provides opportunities to explore and learn in ways that were once unimaginable.

Video games have come a long way since their inception, and the variety of genres available means there is something for everyone. From puzzle games that challenge your problem-solving skills to adventure games that take you on exciting journeys, the possibilities are endless. Many games are designed specifically for older adults, with adjustable difficulty levels and accessible gameplay mechanics to suit a wide range of abilities.

The social aspect of gaming should not be underestimated, as many games offer multiplayer options that allow you to connect with friends, family and fellow gamers from around the world. This can be particularly beneficial in retirement, helping to combat feelings of loneliness and isolation, while fostering a sense of belonging within a supportive gaming community.

In addition to traditional video games, virtual reality (VR) experiences are becoming increasingly popular as a form of entertainment and exploration. Using a VR headset, users can immerse themselves in realistic 3D environments that offer an unprecedented level of interaction and engagement. For retirees, this technology can open up a world of possibilities, from virtual travel and museum tours to interactive art installations and immersive storytelling experiences.

In addition, research has shown that virtual reality and video games can have numerous positive effects on the cognitive function and overall well-being of older adults. Engaging in these activities can help improve memory, attention and even fine motor skills. The stimulating nature of these experiences can also help maintain mental sharpness and a positive outlook on life.

As you embark on your journey into the world of virtual reality and video games, it's important to find experiences that match your interests and abilities. Start by researching popular titles and platforms aimed at retirees, and don't be afraid to ask for recommendations from friends, family or online communities. Remember, the key to enjoying your gaming adventures is to approach them with an open mind and a willingness to learn and adapt to new experiences.

As you explore the world of virtual reality and video games, consider these ideas that can enhance your entertainment experience and provide engaging activities in retirement:

• Virtual Travel: VR experiences like Google Earth VR and Wander allow you to virtually explore famous landmarks, cities, and natural wonders from the comfort of your own home.
• Educational VR Experiences: Titles like The Body VR and Titans of Space offer immersive educational experiences, allowing you to explore human anatomy, the solar system, and more in a visually captivating way.
• Art and Creativity in VR: Programs like Tilt Brush and Quill enable you to create and interact with 3D artwork, providing a unique and expressive creative outlet.
• Social VR Platforms: Apps like VRChat and Rec Room facilitate social interaction in virtual environments, allowing you to connect with friends and make new acquaintances from around the world.
• Brain Training Games: Titles like Lumosity and Brain Age offer a variety of cognitive exercises designed to keep your mind sharp and improve memory, attention, and problem-solving skills.
• Puzzle and Strategy Games: Engaging games like The Witness, Portal, and Civilization VI challenge your critical thinking and planning abilities, offering hours of intellectual stimulation.
• Adventure and Exploration Games: Titles like The Legend of Zelda: Breath of the Wild, Firewatch, and The Elder Scrolls V: Skyrim provide immersive worlds and narratives that you can explore at your own pace.
• Casual and Relaxing Games: Games like Stardew Valley, Animal Crossing, and Journey offer calming and soothing experiences, perfect for unwinding during your leisure time.
• Virtual Reality Fitness: Titles like Beat Saber, BoxVR, and

Supernatural provide fun and engaging workouts in VR, allowing you to stay active and healthy while enjoying immersive gameplay.

• Gaming Consoles for Older Adults: Consider consoles like the Nintendo Switch, which offers a wide variety of accessible and family-friendly games, making it an excellent choice for gamers of all ages.

Creating a Home Theater Experience

Creating a home cinema experience in your retirement years can be a fulfilling and enjoyable project that brings the magic of the cinema right into your living space. Designing and setting up a home theatre not only enhances your entertainment options, but also provides a comfortable and immersive environment in which to relax and unwind.

The first step in creating your home theatre is to choose the right audio and visual equipment to suit your specific needs and preferences. A high-quality TV or projector is essential for crisp, clear images, while a robust sound system ensures you are immersed in rich, immersive audio. When choosing your equipment, consider factors such as screen size, resolution and speaker configuration, as well as your budget and room size.

Designing your room for optimum acoustics and comfort is another important aspect of creating a home cinema experience. For the best sound quality, consider the placement of your speakers and seating in relation to the size and shape of your room. You can also use sound-absorbing materials, such as curtains or carpets, to minimise echo and create a more balanced audio environment.

Comfort is key to enjoying your home cinema, so investing in comfortable seating options such as recliners or plush sofas is essential. You might also consider adding personal touches such as throws, mood lighting or movie-themed decor to create a truly welcoming atmosphere that reflects your unique style and taste.

With your home cinema set up and ready to go, the next step is to explore the various streaming services and content platforms that cater to your entertainment tastes. From movies and TV shows to live sports and concerts, the options are endless, and with the right streaming service, you can curate your own library of on-demand entertainment.

In addition to popular streaming services such as Netflix, Hulu and Amazon Prime Video, you should also consider more specialised platforms that focus on specific genres, such as classic movies or documentaries. This will allow you to discover new content that matches your interests and broaden your cinematic horizons.

Creating a home theatre experience in your retirement can be a rewarding endeavour that not only enhances your entertainment options, but also provides a cosy sanctuary where you can escape from the stresses of everyday life. With careful planning, thoughtful design and the right content selection, your home theatre will quickly become a cherished space where you can enjoy your favourite movies, shows and events in comfort and style.

As you create your home cinema experience, consider these ideas to enhance your entertainment space and make it comfortable, inviting and immersive:

- High quality display: Choose a large-screen TV or projector with excellent resolution for crisp, clear images, taking into account the size of your room and your preferred viewing distance.
- Surround sound system: Invest in a high-quality surround sound system or soundbar that delivers immersive audio to enhance the overall experience of movies, TV shows and games.
- Acoustic treatments: Add sound-absorbing materials such as curtains, carpets or acoustic panels to improve audio quality and minimise echo in your home cinema room.
- Comfortable seating: Opt for cosy seating options such as recliners, plush sofas or even beanbags to ensure you can relax and enjoy your entertainment in comfort.
- Ambient lighting: Consider installing dimmable lights, LED strip lighting or even smart bulbs that can be controlled by your smartphone or voice assistant to create the perfect movie atmosphere.
- Universal remote control: Simplify your home cinema setup with a universal remote that can control all your devices, including your TV, sound system and streaming devices.
- Personalised decor: Add movie-themed decorations, posters or memorabilia to reflect your unique tastes and interests and make your home theatre space feel special.
- Snack station: Set up a snack station or minibar stocked with your favourite treats, popcorn and drinks to enjoy during movie nights or binge-watching sessions.
- Cable management: Keep your home theatre tidy and organised by using cable management solutions such as zip ties, raceways or concealers to hide unsightly wires and cords.
- Streaming Services and Content Platforms: Subscribe to a variety of streaming services such as Netflix, Hulu or Amazon Prime Video, as well as more specialised genre-focused platforms, to access a vast library of

on-demand entertainment.

Discovering New Music, Podcasts, and Audiobooks

Discovering new music, podcasts and audiobooks in retirement can be a wonderful way to broaden your horizons and enrich your daily life. With the vast array of audio entertainment available today, there are endless opportunities to find content that resonates with your interests, piques your curiosity and provides a soundtrack to your leisure activities.

One of the joys of retirement is having the time and freedom to explore new musical genres and artists. By venturing beyond your usual listening preferences, you can gain a deeper appreciation for the diverse world of music and even discover hidden gems that speak to your soul. Whether it's attending live concerts, exploring music streaming services or connecting with like-minded music lovers, immersing yourself in the world of music can be a rewarding and inspiring experience.

Podcasts have become an increasingly popular form of audio entertainment, offering an intimate and engaging way to learn about a wide range of topics. From true crime stories and history lessons to personal growth and comedy, there is a podcast for every interest and taste. By incorporating podcasts into your daily routine, you can stay informed, entertained and connected to the world around you. In addition, podcasts often feature interviews and discussions with experts, thought leaders and other interesting personalities, providing unique perspectives and insights that can enrich your understanding of various topics.

Audiobooks are another form of audio entertainment and can be a particularly enjoyable way to experience literature in retirement. Whether you're revisiting classic novels or exploring contemporary bestsellers, audiobooks allow you to immerse yourself in compelling stories and ideas while enjoying the convenience and flexibility of a hands-free format. This can be particularly useful for multitasking, as you can listen to an audiobook while engaging in other activities such as walking, gardening or even cooking.

In addition to the entertainment value, discovering new music, podcasts and audiobooks can have numerous cognitive and emotional benefits for retirees. Engaging with diverse audio content can stimulate the mind, promote mental acuity and foster a sense of connection to the wider world. In addition, the act of discovering and sharing new audio content with friends and family can lead to lively discussions and meaningful interactions that strengthen your bonds and deepen your relationships.

As you embark on your journey to discover new music, podcasts and audiobooks, it's important to explore different platforms and resources that cater to your specific interests and preferences. This may include browsing popular streaming services, seeking recommendations from friends and family, or joining online communities dedicated to your favourite genres. By staying curious and open to new experiences, you can make your retirement a rich and fulfilling time of personal growth, discovery and connection.

As you explore new music, podcasts, and audiobooks, consider these ideas to help you discover a wealth of diverse and engaging content to enjoy during your retirement:

• Music streaming services: Platforms like Spotify, Apple Music, and Tidal offer personalized playlists and recommendations based on your listening habits, helping you discover new artists and genres.
• Music discovery apps: Apps like Shazam and SoundHound can help you identify songs you hear in public or on the radio, making it easy to find and save new music you enjoy.
• Podcast directories: Browse popular podcast directories like Apple Podcasts, Google Podcasts, and Stitcher, where you can search for podcasts by genre, popularity, or specific interests.
• Podcast recommendations: Ask friends, family, or online communities for podcast suggestions, or follow the social media accounts of your favorite podcast hosts to stay updated on new episodes and recommendations.
• Audiobook platforms: Subscribe to services like Audible or Libby, which offer a vast library of audiobooks across various genres, including new releases, bestsellers, and classics.
• Online music communities: Join forums, Facebook groups, or subreddit communities dedicated to specific genres, artists, or music-related topics, where you can discuss and discover new music with like-minded individuals.
• Live music streaming and virtual concerts: Attend virtual concerts, live streams, or music festivals online to experience live music and discover new artists from the comfort of your home.
• Radio shows and playlists: Tune in to radio shows or curated playlists on platforms like BBC Radio, NPR Music, or Pandora, which often feature interviews, live performances, and new music discoveries.
• Book clubs and online reading communities: Join book clubs, online forums, or social media groups dedicated to discussing literature and sharing audiobook recommendations.
• Local events and workshops: Attend local events, workshops, or meetups focused on music, podcasting, or literature to connect with

others who share your interests and discover new content through discussions and recommendations.

FUN WITH FAMILY AND FRIENDS

Enjoying family and friends in retirement is an essential part of maintaining strong relationships and living a fulfilling life. By making the most of your newfound free time, you can deepen your connections with loved ones and create lasting memories.

Organising family reunions and get-togethers can be a wonderful way to reconnect with relatives you may not have seen for some time. By planning these gatherings carefully, you can create an atmosphere that encourages everyone to share stories, reminisce about shared memories and strengthen family bonds. These events are an excellent opportunity to celebrate your unique family history and traditions and ensure that they are passed down through the generations.

Activities such as board game and jigsaw puzzle nights offer the chance to bond with loved ones through friendly competition and laughter. These events can bring people of all ages together and provide a fun and inclusive environment for everyone to enjoy. By choosing a variety of board games and puzzles to suit different interests and skill levels, you can ensure that everyone feels included and engaged.

Film and TV marathons can be a cosy and entertaining way to spend time with family and friends. By choosing films and series that appeal to a range of tastes, you can create an enjoyable experience for everyone. These marathons can be enhanced with themed snacks, decorations or activities to create a more immersive and memorable event.

Hosting theme parties and potlucks allows you to bring your loved ones together in a festive and creative environment. By choosing a fun theme for your get-together, you can encourage your guests to dress up, prepare themed food and participate in related activities. These events not only create a lively atmosphere, but also provide a platform for sharing experiences and stories.

Exploring local festivals and events with your family and friends can be a great way to enrich your retirement years. By attending cultural events, food festivals and community gatherings, you can discover new experiences, learn about different traditions and foster a sense of belonging within your community. These outings can also be a wonderful way to bond with loved ones over shared interests and create lasting memories.

As you move through your retirement years, making the most of your time with family and friends can greatly enhance your overall happiness and well-being. By planning and participating in a variety of activities and events, you can deepen your relationships, share new experiences and create a rich and fulfilling life.

Organizing Family Reunions and Get-Togethers

Organising family reunions and get-togethers in retirement can be a wonderful way to strengthen family bonds, create cherished memories and celebrate your unique family history. These events provide an opportunity to bring together relatives who may have lost touch or live far away, helping to maintain and deepen connections across generations.

When planning a family reunion or gathering, it's important to consider everyone's needs and preferences to ensure everyone feels welcome and included. Choosing a convenient location that is easily accessible to all family members is an important first step. Depending on the size of your group and the atmosphere you want to create, you may choose a central meeting place such as a park, a rented venue or even a family member's home.

To make the event enjoyable and memorable for everyone, consider organising activities that appeal to different age groups and interests. Activities such as storytelling, talent shows or family quizzes can build a sense of camaraderie and fun. In addition, incorporating your family's unique cultural or regional traditions, whether through food, music or shared customs, can create a more meaningful and personal experience.

Communication is key when organising a family reunion or gathering. Make sure all family members are well informed about the details of the event, including the date, location and any planned activities. You can set up a dedicated group chat, social media page or even a website to keep everyone updated and facilitate communication. It's also important to remain open to feedback and suggestions from family members to ensure that everyone feels heard and involved in the planning process.

Another important aspect of organising a family reunion or gathering is to ensure that everyone has an opportunity to contribute. This can be done by delegating tasks such as food preparation, decorating or organising activities to different family members. Encouraging everyone to participate not only helps to spread responsibility, but also promotes a sense of ownership and pride in the event.

Organising family reunions and get-togethers in retirement can be a very rewarding experience. By taking the time to plan these events thoughtfully, you can create an environment that fosters connection, shared memories and a celebration of your unique family history.

Simple ideas:

• Memory Lane: Encourage family members to bring old photos, memorabilia, and family heirlooms to create a "Memory Lane" display during the reunion.
• Family Tree: Create a family tree together, with each family member contributing information about their branch of the family. This can be a great conversation starter and help everyone learn more about their family history.
• Talent Show: Organize a family talent show where everyone can showcase their unique skills, from singing and dancing to magic tricks or stand-up comedy.
• Group Activities: Plan group activities like scavenger hunts, relay races, or team-building games that encourage interaction and teamwork among family members.
• Themed Reunions: Choose a theme for the reunion, such as a specific decade, culture, or family tradition, and encourage everyone to dress accordingly and bring themed food and decorations.
• Family Cookbook: Ask each family member to contribute a favorite recipe to compile a family cookbook that can be distributed as a keepsake after the reunion.
• DIY Photo Booth: Set up a DIY photo booth with fun props and backdrops for family members to take group pictures and create lasting memories.
• Family Trivia: Create a family trivia game with questions about family history, anecdotes, and fun facts about each family member.
• Storytelling: Organize a storytelling session where family members can share personal stories, anecdotes, and family legends with one another.
• Family T-Shirt: Design a custom family t-shirt for everyone to wear during the reunion, featuring the family name, reunion date, or a fun family slogan.
• Charitable Project: Plan a charitable project, such as volunteering at a local food bank or organizing a donation drive, that the whole family can participate in together.
• Movie Night: Host a family movie night, featuring films that are significant to your family or films starring relatives who have been involved in the entertainment industry.
• Family Olympics: Organize a "Family Olympics" with various games and competitions that family members can participate in, complete with a medal ceremony at the end.

- Time Capsule: Create a family time capsule with letters, photos, and mementos from the reunion to be opened at a future family gathering.
- Cultural Celebration: Organize a reunion that celebrates your family's cultural heritage, featuring traditional food, music, and activities.

Board Game and Puzzle Nights

Board game and puzzle nights are a great way to bond with family and friends in retirement. These engaging and entertaining events can bring people of all ages together, creating an inclusive and enjoyable environment that encourages conversation, laughter and friendly competition. With a wide variety of board games and puzzles to choose from, there is sure to be something for everyone, making these evenings a fantastic opportunity to reconnect with loved ones and create cherished memories.

One of the key elements of a successful board game and jigsaw night is choosing the right games and puzzles to suit the interests and skill levels of everyone. By selecting a variety of options, you can ensure that everyone has the opportunity to participate and enjoy themselves. From classic board games such as Monopoly, Scrabble or Chess to more modern and innovative games such as Catan or Codenames, there are plenty of options to suit any group.

In addition to board games, jigsaw puzzles can also provide a fun and engaging activity for your game nights. Jigsaw puzzles, crossword puzzles and brain teasers are all great ways to exercise your mind and work with others to solve challenges. These activities can be particularly enjoyable for those who prefer a quieter or more contemplative game night experience.

Creating a comfortable and welcoming atmosphere is another important aspect of running successful board game and jigsaw puzzle nights. Make sure there is enough seating and table space for everyone to participate comfortably, and consider offering snacks and drinks to keep everyone refreshed and energised. Soft lighting and background music can also help create a cosy and relaxed environment that encourages conversation and connection.

To keep your board game and puzzle nights fresh and exciting, consider introducing new games and puzzles on a regular basis, or inviting guest players to join your group. This can help maintain interest and enthusiasm, as well as providing an opportunity to learn new games and strategies from others.

Board game and puzzle nights in retirement can be a fun and rewarding way to bond with family and friends. By carefully selecting a range of games and puzzles, creating a welcoming atmosphere and ensuring that everyone has the opportunity to participate and enjoy themselves, you can create lasting memories and strengthen relationships with your loved ones.

Simple ideas:

• Mystery Night: Choose a selection of detective-themed board games and puzzles, like Clue or Sherlock Holmes Consulting Detective, for an evening of mystery-solving fun.
• Strategy Games: Focus on strategy games like Settlers of Catan, Risk, or Ticket to Ride, which encourage critical thinking and competition among players.
• Classic Board Game Night: Bring out the classic board games, such as Monopoly, Scrabble, and Trivial Pursuit, for a nostalgic evening of friendly competition.
• Puzzle Party: Set up multiple jigsaw puzzles with varying levels of difficulty around the room and let guests work together or individually to complete them.
• Escape Room Night: Create an at-home escape room experience using puzzle games like Exit: The Game or Unlock! Adventures, challenging guests to solve riddles and decipher clues to "escape" within a set time.
• Trivia Night: Host a trivia night with board games like Wits & Wagers or Bezzerwizzer, testing guests' knowledge in various categories.
• Cooperative Game Night: Choose cooperative board games like Pandemic, Forbidden Island, or Flash Point: Fire Rescue, where players must work together to achieve a common goal.
• DIY Board Game: Encourage guests to design and create their own board games or puzzles to share with the group, sparking creativity and collaboration.
• Couples Game Night: Invite couples to compete against each other in team-based board games or puzzles, fostering friendly competition and teamwork.
• Board Game Tournament: Organize a board game tournament, where players compete in multiple games throughout the evening and earn points based on their performance. Crown a champion at the end of the night.
• Themed Game Night: Choose a theme for the evening, such as space, fantasy, or adventure, and select board games and puzzles that align with that theme.
• Blind Game Night: Wrap the board games in plain paper and have guests choose a game at random, adding an element of surprise and discovery to the evening.
• Educational Game Night: Focus on educational games, such as

Timeline or BrainBox, that teach players about history, science, or other subjects while providing entertainment.
- Speed Puzzle Night: Set a timer and challenge guests to complete puzzles as quickly as possible, either individually or in teams.
- Game Night Potluck: Ask each guest to bring their favorite board game or puzzle, creating a diverse and exciting selection for everyone to enjoy.

Movie and TV Show Marathons

Movie and TV show marathons are a fantastic way to bond with family and friends in retirement. By planning these marathons and carefully selecting films or series that appeal to a variety of tastes, you can create a cosy and entertaining atmosphere that brings your loved ones together. These marathons can be a great way to revisit beloved classics, discover new favourites, or simply enjoy the company of those closest to you while indulging in the magic of the big screen.

When planning a film or TV marathon, it's important to consider your guests' preferences to ensure everyone feels included and engaged. You can choose a mix of genres such as action, comedy, drama or romance to cater for a wide range of interests. Alternatively, you could choose a theme for your marathon, such as films from a particular decade, films by a particular director, or a TV series that everyone in your group enjoys.

Creating a comfortable and inviting environment is crucial for a successful film or TV marathon. Make sure there is plenty of seating with cushions and blankets to create a cosy atmosphere. Dimming the lights and adjusting the room temperature can also enhance the overall experience and make it more enjoyable for everyone.

To make your film or TV marathon even more memorable, consider incorporating themed snacks or decorations that complement the films or series you've chosen. For example, if you're hosting a marathon of classic Hollywood films, you could serve popcorn in vintage containers or decorate your room with vintage movie posters. This attention to detail can help create a more immersive and enjoyable experience for your guests.

During the marathon, be sure to schedule breaks for your guests to stretch, use the restroom, or simply chat with one another. These breaks can be a great way to encourage conversation and allow everyone to share their thoughts on the films or series they've watched. You may even want to consider a post-marathon discussion or quiz session to keep your guests engaged and create lasting memories.

Movie and TV show marathons can be a wonderful way to spend quality time with family and friends during retirement. By carefully selecting films or series that appeal to a range of tastes, creating a comfortable and inviting environment, and adding thoughtful touches such as themed snacks or decorations, you can create a memorable event that everyone will cherish.

Simple ideas:
- Genre Marathon: Choose a specific genre, such as action, comedy, or romance, and create a marathon lineup featuring movies or TV shows within that genre.
- Director or Actor Spotlight: Focus on a specific director or actor, showcasing their most iconic works or lesser-known gems.
- Award Winners: Host a marathon of critically acclaimed films or TV shows that have won prestigious awards, such as Oscars or Emmys.
- Franchise Marathon: Choose a popular film or TV franchise, like Star Wars, Harry Potter, or The Marvel Cinematic Universe, and watch them in chronological order.
- Decade Marathon: Select movies or TV shows from a specific decade, allowing guests to reminisce and appreciate the styles, trends, and themes of that era.
- Foreign Film Night: Organize a marathon of foreign films or TV shows, introducing guests to different cultures, languages, and storytelling styles.
- Animated Marathon: Choose a lineup of animated movies or TV shows, from classic Disney films to modern-day Pixar or Studio Ghibli masterpieces.
- Guilty Pleasures: Encourage guests to share their favorite "guilty pleasure" movies or TV shows, creating a fun and lighthearted marathon lineup.
- Cult Classics: Host a marathon of cult classic films or TV shows, such as The Rocky Horror Picture Show or Twin Peaks, that have amassed dedicated fan followings.
- Binge-Worthy TV Series: Select a highly addictive TV series, like Breaking Bad or Stranger Things, and watch multiple episodes or even entire seasons in one sitting.
- Documentary Marathon: Choose a selection of intriguing documentaries, covering various topics such as nature, history, or true crime.
- Holiday-Themed Marathon: Organize a marathon of movies or TV specials centered around a specific holiday, like Christmas, Halloween, or Valentine's Day.
- Musical Marathon: Create a lineup of movie or TV musicals,

encouraging guests to sing along to their favorite tunes.

• Movie Adaptations: Host a marathon of movies or TV shows based on popular books or plays, comparing the adaptations to their original source material.

• Science Fiction and Fantasy: Organize a marathon of sci-fi and fantasy films or TV shows, transporting guests to imaginative worlds and alternate realities.

Hosting Theme Parties and Potlucks

Hosting theme parties and potlucks in retirement can be a wonderful way to bring family and friends together to share good food, conversation and laughter. By choosing a fun and creative theme for your get-together, you can encourage your guests to express themselves through what they wear, the dishes they prepare and the activities they take part in. These events not only create a lively atmosphere, but also provide a platform for sharing experiences and stories, helping to strengthen your relationships with your loved ones.

When planning a theme party or potluck, the first step is to choose a theme that will resonate with your group and generate excitement and enthusiasm. This can be anything from a decade or holiday to a cultural celebration or even a favourite movie or TV show. The key is to choose a theme that gives your guests plenty of opportunity to get creative with their outfits, food and decorations.

Once you've chosen a theme, it's important to let your guests know the details well in advance so they have plenty of time to prepare. This could include sending out invitations with clear instructions about the theme, dress code and any special dishes or items they should bring. Be sure to include the date, time and location of the event, as well as any other relevant details that will help your guests plan their attendance.

As well as dressing up and bringing themed food, you can also include activities and entertainment that tie in with your chosen theme. This could include organising games, quizzes or even a talent show that encourages guests to show off their skills or knowledge related to the theme. These activities can add an extra layer of fun and engagement to your event, helping to create a memorable and enjoyable experience for everyone.

Creating a welcoming and festive atmosphere is another important aspect of a successful theme party or potluck. Decorate your space with themed items such as banners, tableware or even DIY decorations that reflect your chosen theme. This attention to detail can help create an immersive and visually appealing environment that will delight your guests and set the stage for a fantastic get-together.

Be sure to capture the memories of your theme party or potluck by taking plenty of photos and videos throughout the event. This will not only provide you with treasured keepsakes to look back on, but will also allow your guests to reminisce about the fun and laughter they shared with you during this special occasion.

Simple ideas:

- Decade Party: Choose a specific decade, such as the '80s or '90s, and encourage guests to dress in period-appropriate attire while serving food and playing music from that era.
- Costume Party: Organize a costume party with a specific theme, such as superheroes, famous celebrities, or movie characters, and encourage guests to dress up accordingly.
- Around the World Potluck: Ask each guest to bring a dish from a different country or culture, allowing everyone to taste and appreciate diverse cuisines.
- Movie or TV Show Theme: Host a party centered around a popular movie or TV show, with themed decorations, costumes, and dishes inspired by the chosen film or series.
- Color-Themed Party: Choose a specific color for the theme, and encourage guests to wear clothing in that color and bring dishes that correspond with the chosen hue.
- Murder Mystery Dinner: Organize a murder mystery party where guests play characters and work together to solve a fictional crime while enjoying a potluck dinner.
- Game Night Potluck: Combine a potluck with a game night, asking each guest to bring their favorite dish and board game to share with the group.
- Outdoor BBQ Party: Host an outdoor barbecue party with a specific theme, such as a luau or a country western cookout, complete with themed decorations and activities.
- Masquerade Ball: Organize a formal masquerade party with guests wearing masks and elegant attire, while serving fancy appetizers and cocktails.
- Progressive Dinner Party: Coordinate with neighbors or friends to host a progressive dinner party, where guests move from one house to another for different courses of a meal.
- Seasonal Celebration: Host a theme party centered around a specific season, like a summer beach bash, a fall harvest festival, or a winter wonderland

- Sports Party: Organize a party based on a popular sport or a big game, with themed decorations, team-colored attire, and snacks inspired by stadium food.
- DIY Pizza Party: Set up a DIY pizza station with various toppings, allowing guests to create their own personalized pizzas while socializing and enjoying each other's company.
- Talent Show Party: Invite guests to showcase their unique skills or hobbies in a talent show, while enjoying a potluck spread of everyone's favorite dishes.
- Brunch Party: Host a themed brunch party, such as a pajama party or a garden party, and encourage guests to bring their favorite breakfast or brunch dishes to share.

Attending Local Festivals and Events

Attending local festivals and events in retirement can be a fantastic way to immerse yourself in your community, explore new experiences and create lasting memories with family and friends. By attending these events, you can learn about different cultures, enjoy a variety of performances and activities, and discover new interests or hobbies that can enrich your life in retirement.

Local festivals and events offer a variety of experiences to suit a wide range of interests and preferences. These can include cultural celebrations, food and wine festivals, music or film festivals, art exhibitions or even community fundraisers and charity events. By attending these events, you can gain a deeper understanding of your community and the people who live in it, fostering a sense of belonging and connection.

One of the main benefits of attending local festivals and events is the opportunity to meet new people and expand your social circle. These gatherings provide a welcoming and inclusive environment where you can strike up conversations, share experiences and make new friends. This can be particularly valuable in retirement, helping to maintain your social wellbeing and prevent feelings of isolation or loneliness.

Another benefit of attending local festivals and events is the possibility of discovering new interests or hobbies that you may not have considered before. For example, you might attend a local art festival and be inspired to take up painting, or attend a food festival and develop a passion for cooking. By remaining open and curious, you can continue to learn and grow throughout your retirement years, contributing to your overall happiness and well-being.

As well as enriching your own life, attending local festivals and events can have a positive impact on your community. By supporting these gatherings, you contribute to the local economy, help promote local talent and culture, and foster a sense of unity and pride within your community. This can lead to a more vibrant and thriving neighbourhood, which in turn benefits everyone who lives there.

Simple ideas:

- Food Festivals: Attend local food festivals featuring regional cuisine, street food, and specialty vendors.
- Art Fairs: Attend local art fairs and craft shows featuring works from local artisans and artists.
- Music Festivals: Attend local music festivals featuring a variety of genres and artists, from up-and-coming indie bands to well-known headliners.
- Cultural Celebrations: Attend local cultural celebrations, such as parades, festivals, and fairs, highlighting different ethnicities, traditions, and customs.
- Sporting Events: Attend local sporting events, such as minor league baseball games or high school football games, and cheer on the local teams.
- Farmers Markets: Attend local farmers markets, featuring fresh produce, artisanal goods, and locally made products.
- Film Festivals: Attend local film festivals, showcasing a variety of independent films, short films, and documentaries.
- Street Fairs: Attend local street fairs featuring food vendors, artisanal crafts, live music, and other forms of entertainment.
- Historical Reenactments: Attend local historical reenactments, offering a glimpse into local history and culture.
- Nature Walks: Attend local nature walks, guided hikes, and nature-themed events to explore the natural beauty of the area.
- Beer and Wine Festivals: Attend local beer and wine festivals, featuring local breweries and wineries and offering tastings and other fun activities.
- Car Shows: Attend local car shows, featuring classic cars, hot rods, and other unique vehicles.
- Holiday Festivals: Attend local holiday festivals, featuring tree lightings, parades, and other seasonal activities.
- Charity Events: Attend local charity events, such as benefit concerts or fundraising walks, to support local causes and organizations.
- Outdoor Concerts: Attend local outdoor concerts and music events, featuring local bands and musicians, and enjoy the warm weather and beautiful surroundings.

Game Nights with Friends and Family

Game nights with friends and family in retirement can be a wonderful way to spend quality time together, creating an atmosphere of fun, laughter and friendly competition. These gatherings provide an opportunity for people of all ages to connect and bond over a shared activity, strengthening relationships and fostering a sense of camaraderie. Whether you prefer traditional board games, card games or video games, game nights can provide hours of entertainment and fun for everyone involved.

One of the most important aspects of running a successful game night is choosing the right games for your group. This means considering the interests and skill levels of your guests and choosing a mix of games to suit different tastes. By offering a variety of options, you can ensure that everyone has the opportunity to participate and enjoy themselves, regardless of their experience or preferences.

As well as choosing the right games, it's also important to create a welcoming and comfortable environment for your guests. This includes providing plenty of seating and table space, as well as refreshments to keep everyone energised and engaged throughout the evening. You might also consider adjusting the lighting and playing background music to create a more relaxed and enjoyable atmosphere.

To keep your game nights fresh and exciting, consider rotating the games you play or introducing new ones on a regular basis. This can help maintain interest and enthusiasm among your guests, as well as providing an opportunity to learn new skills and strategies. You might also consider inviting guest players or organising friendly tournaments to add an extra element of fun and challenge to your game nights.

Another important aspect of hosting game nights with friends and family is to ensure that the atmosphere remains light-hearted and inclusive. Encourage good sportsmanship, laughter and friendly banter, but also make sure you maintain a positive and supportive environment for all players. This can help create a more enjoyable experience for everyone and ensure that your game nights continue to be a cherished tradition among your loved ones.

Simple ideas:

• Classic Board Game Night: Play classic board games like Monopoly, Scrabble, and Clue, providing a fun and nostalgic way to connect with friends and family.

- Trivia Night: Host a trivia night with different categories, such as history, pop culture, and sports, allowing everyone to showcase their knowledge and compete for prizes.
- Card Game Night: Play classic card games, like poker, blackjack, and bridge, or newer games like Cards Against Humanity or Exploding Kittens, for a night of fun and laughs.
- Video Game Night: Play video games together, whether on a console, computer, or mobile device, enjoying multiplayer games and friendly competition.
- Role-Playing Game Night: Play role-playing games, like Dungeons & Dragons, allowing players to create their own characters and embark on exciting quests and adventures.
- Puzzle Night: Work on jigsaw puzzles together, either individually or as a group, providing a relaxing and engaging activity for all ages.
- Party Game Night: Play party games, like charades, Pictionary, or Taboo, encouraging creativity, communication, and laughter.
- Group Strategy Games: Play group strategy games, like Settlers of Catan or Risk, fostering critical thinking, communication, and teamwork among players.
- Escape Room Night: Create an at-home escape room experience using puzzle games like Exit: The Game or Unlock! Adventures, challenging players to solve riddles and decipher clues to "escape" within a set time.
- Classic Arcade Night: Set up classic arcade games, like Pac-Man or Space Invaders, providing a fun and retro gaming experience for everyone.
- Tabletop Games: Play tabletop games, such as Warhammer, Magic: The Gathering, or Settlers of Catan, allowing players to immerse themselves in complex and engaging worlds.
- Minute-to-Win-It Night: Play games that require quick thinking and fast reflexes, such as Minute-to-Win-It challenges or speed stacking competitions.
- Scavenger Hunt Night: Organize a scavenger hunt, either indoors or outdoors, providing a fun and exciting way to explore and discover new things together.
- Virtual Game Night: Play games online, such as Jackbox Games or Among Us, connecting with friends and family virtually and enjoying multiplayer games from the comfort of your own homes.
- Sports Night: Play sports-themed games, such as foosball or ping pong, providing a fun and active way to connect with friends and family.

Movie and Theatre Outings

Cinema and theatre trips in retirement are a fantastic way to enjoy the arts, immerse yourself in compelling stories and share these experiences with your loved ones. By attending a variety of performances and screenings, you can explore new genres, discover emerging talent and appreciate the creativity and skill that goes into producing these works. In addition, these outings can be an excellent opportunity to socialise and connect with your friends and family, fostering shared memories and a sense of togetherness.

One of the benefits of film and theatre trips is that they expose you to a wide range of artistic expressions, from independent films and documentaries to Broadway productions and local theatre performances. By being open to new experiences and stepping outside your comfort zone, you can gain a deeper appreciation for the arts and possibly discover new favourites that you may not have otherwise encountered.

When planning a cinema or theatre outing, it's important to consider the tastes and interests of the people in your party. This could mean researching upcoming shows and screenings, reading reviews, or getting recommendations from friends and family to find events that will appeal to everyone in your group. By choosing from a variety of options, you can cater to different tastes and ensure that everyone has an enjoyable experience.

To make your film and theatre outings even more memorable, consider including pre- or post-show activities, such as dining at a nearby restaurant or attending a talkback session with the cast or filmmakers. These additional elements can enhance the overall experience and provide opportunities for conversation and engagement with the works you've just seen.

Another aspect to consider when planning film and theatre outings is accessibility and convenience. Consider the needs of your companions and choose venues that are easily accessible and offer comfortable seating and amenities. This will ensure that everyone can fully enjoy the experience without unnecessary discomfort or inconvenience.

Simple ideas:

- Classic Movie Night: Attend a screening of a classic movie at a local theater or a revival cinema, offering the opportunity to experience beloved films on the big screen.
- New Release Movie Night: Attend a screening of a new release movie

at a local theater, enjoying the latest blockbusters or critically acclaimed films.
- Independent Film Night: Attend a screening of an independent film at an arthouse cinema, supporting emerging filmmakers and discovering unique stories and perspectives.
- Outdoor Movie Night: Attend an outdoor movie screening, either at a local park or a drive-in theater, enjoying movies under the stars with blankets, snacks, and drinks.
- Dinner and a Movie Night: Enjoy dinner at a restaurant before or after attending a movie, providing a fun and relaxing date night or a night out with friends.
- Broadway Show: Attend a Broadway show or musical, experiencing the excitement and spectacle of live theater.
- Local Theater: Attend a play or performance at a local theater, supporting the local arts community and discovering new talents and productions.
- Improv Night: Attend an improv comedy show, laughing and enjoying spontaneous performances by talented comedians.
- Film Festival: Attend a film festival, showcasing a variety of independent films, short films, and documentaries, providing the opportunity to discover new and emerging talents.
- Silent Movie Night: Attend a silent movie screening, either at a local theater or a silent film festival, enjoying classic films accompanied by live music or sound effects.
- Movie Concert: Attend a movie concert, where a live orchestra performs the soundtrack to a classic movie, providing a unique and immersive experience.
- Opera or Ballet: Attend an opera or ballet performance, experiencing the beauty and grace of these timeless art forms.
- Comedy Show: Attend a stand-up comedy show, enjoying the wit and humor of popular comedians or up-and-coming talents.
- Film Talk: Attend a film talk or discussion, featuring filmmakers, actors, or critics, providing the opportunity to learn more about the art and craft of filmmaking.
- Movie Trivia Night: Attend a movie trivia night at a local bar or theater, testing your knowledge of film trivia and competing with other movie enthusiasts.

Potlucks, Picnics, and Social Gatherings

Retirement potlucks, picnics and get-togethers are a wonderful way to bring family and friends together to share food, conversation and laughter. These events can be held in a variety of settings, from your own backyard to a local park or community centre, and can be tailored to the preferences and interests of your guests. By hosting or attending these gatherings, you can maintain strong connections with loved ones, meet new people, and create lasting memories that will enrich your retirement years.

Potlucks are a popular choice for social gatherings because they encourage everyone to contribute a dish and share the responsibility of providing the food. This allows guests to show off their culinary skills and share their favourite recipes, resulting in a diverse and delicious array of dishes for everyone to enjoy. When organising a potluck, it's important to communicate any dietary restrictions or preferences of your guests so that everyone can be accommodated and feel included.

Picnics are another enjoyable way to spend time with friends and family in retirement, combining the pleasures of al fresco dining with the opportunity to enjoy nature and fresh air. When planning a picnic, be sure to choose a location with plenty of shade, seating and facilities such as toilets and playgrounds if needed. Pack a variety of foods that are easy to carry and share, and don't forget the essentials such as cutlery, napkins and drinks.

Social gatherings can take many forms, from informal get-togethers at home to more structured events such as themed parties or holiday celebrations. The key to a successful social gathering is to create a welcoming and comfortable atmosphere that encourages conversation and interaction among your guests. This can include arranging seating to encourage mingling, choosing appropriate background music and offering a variety of food and drink options to suit different tastes.

In addition to nurturing your existing relationships, potlucks, picnics and social gatherings can also be an opportunity to expand your social circle and meet new people. By inviting neighbours, acquaintances or members of local clubs or organisations to your events, you can expand your network of friends and enrich your retirement years with new connections and experiences.

Retirement potlucks, picnics and social gatherings can be a rewarding and enjoyable way to maintain strong connections with loved ones, discover new interests and create lasting memories. By hosting or participating in these events, you can contribute to a fulfilling and engaging retirement experience for yourself and those around you.

Simple ideas:

- Backyard BBQ: Host a backyard barbecue, providing a fun and casual

way to enjoy delicious food, drinks, and conversation with friends and family
- Picnic in the Park: Organize a picnic in a local park or a scenic spot, enjoying the outdoors and sharing food and drinks with others.
- Potluck Party: Host a potluck party, inviting guests to bring their favorite dishes and sharing a variety of food and drinks, providing a fun and communal dining experience.
- Brunch Gathering: Host a brunch gathering, serving delicious breakfast foods and drinks, providing a casual and relaxed atmosphere for socializing with friends and family.
- Wine and Cheese Night: Host a wine and cheese night, serving a variety of cheeses and wines, providing a sophisticated and enjoyable way to socialize with others.
- Cocktail Party: Host a cocktail party, serving delicious cocktails and appetizers, providing a sophisticated and fun way to entertain guests.
- Karaoke Party: Host a karaoke party, providing a fun and lively way to sing and dance with friends and family, and enjoying food and drinks.
- Ice Cream Social: Host an ice cream social, providing a sweet and refreshing way to socialize with others and enjoy various ice cream flavors and toppings.
- Cook-Off Competition: Host a cook-off competition, inviting guests to bring and share their best recipes and compete for prizes, providing a fun and competitive way to socialize and enjoy delicious food.

EDUCATIONAL PURSUITS

Retirement is often seen as a time to relax and enjoy the fruits of one's labour, but it can also be an opportunity for continued personal growth and development. One way to achieve this is through educational pursuits. Whether it's learning a new skill or delving deeper into a favourite subject, there are many options for retirees looking to broaden their horizons.

One of the most popular educational pursuits for retirees is online learning. With the advent of technology, online courses and webinars have become increasingly accessible and convenient. From language learning apps to university-level courses, online learning offers a wide range of options for retirees looking to learn new skills or explore new topics.

Another great way to pursue educational interests is to visit museums and art galleries. These institutions offer a wealth of knowledge and inspiration, from ancient history to contemporary art. Many museums and galleries also offer guided tours and workshops, making the learning experience more interactive and engaging.

Science and technology fairs are another great way to stay informed and educated in retirement. These events showcase the latest innovations and advances in science and technology, providing a hands-on and interactive way to learn about new discoveries and breakthroughs.

For retirees who enjoy competition and trivia, taking part in quizzes and trivia nights can be a fun and engaging way to test their knowledge and learn new facts. These events are often held in local bars and restaurants and offer prizes for the winners.

Attending lectures and workshops is another great way for retirees to stay engaged and informed. Many universities, libraries and community centres offer lectures and workshops on a wide range of topics, from history and politics to science and technology. These events give retirees the opportunity to learn from experts and engage in lively discussions with their peers.

Learning a new language is also a popular educational activity for retirees. Not only does it provide an opportunity to interact with people from different cultures, but it also promotes cognitive health and improves memory and problem-solving skills. There are many language learning resources available online, including language learning apps, online courses and language exchange programmes.

Researching genealogy and family history is another educational activity that can be both fascinating and rewarding. With the help of genealogy websites and resources, retirees can research their family tree and uncover interesting stories and connections to the past.

Enrolling in continuing education courses is also a great way for retirees to pursue educational interests and learn new skills. Many universities and community colleges offer continuing education courses for retirees and seniors on topics ranging from cooking and photography to history and literature.

Educational pursuits are a great way for retirees to stay engaged, informed and inspired. From online learning to museum visits and quizzes, there are many options for retirees looking to broaden their horizons and continue their personal growth and development.

Online Courses and Webinars

Online courses and webinars have become increasingly popular in recent years, providing a convenient and accessible way for people of all ages and backgrounds to learn new skills and expand their knowledge. This is especially true for retirees, who often have more free time and want to pursue educational interests in their golden years.

One of the main advantages of online courses and webinars is their flexibility. Unlike traditional classroom-based courses, online courses can be taken from anywhere, at any time. This makes them an ideal choice for retirees who may have travel plans or other commitments that make attending regular classes difficult. Online courses also allow learners to work at their own pace, so they can spend more time on more challenging topics or move more quickly through easier material.

Another advantage of online courses and webinars is their affordability. Many online courses are offered for free or at low cost, making them accessible to learners on a budget. This is especially important for retirees who may be living on a fixed income and want to continue learning without breaking the bank.

Online courses and webinars also offer a wide range of topics and subjects to choose from. From business and technology to art and history, there is no shortage of options for retirees looking to expand their knowledge and skills. Many courses are also taught by experts in their field, providing learners with high-quality instruction and insight.

One of the greatest benefits of online courses and webinars is the opportunity they provide for lifelong learning. Retirement is often seen as a time to slow down and relax, but for many retirees it can also be an opportunity for continued personal growth and development. Online courses and webinars offer a convenient and accessible way to pursue educational interests and learn new skills, promoting cognitive health and keeping the mind sharp and active.

Online courses and webinars provide a convenient and accessible way for retirees to pursue educational interests and expand their knowledge and skills. Their flexibility, affordability and wide range of topics and subjects make them an ideal choice for retirees who want to continue learning and staying engaged in their golden years.

Here are some examples of online courses and webinars that retirees may find interesting and engaging:

- Creative Writing: Many online courses and webinars are available to help retirees improve their creative writing skills. These courses can include classes on memoir writing, fiction writing, or poetry.
- Financial Planning: Online courses and webinars are available to help retirees manage their finances and plan for retirement. These courses can include topics such as retirement income planning, estate planning, and investment strategies.
- Language Learning: Language learning courses are available online for retirees who want to learn a new language or refresh their language skills. These courses can include classes in Spanish, French, Mandarin, or other languages.
- Historical Studies: Many online courses and webinars are available to help retirees learn about history and culture. These courses can include classes on ancient civilizations, world history, or local history.
- Health and Wellness: Online courses and webinars are available to help retirees maintain their health and wellness. These courses can include topics such as nutrition, exercise, meditation, and stress management.
- Technology and Social Media: Online courses and webinars can help retirees learn about new technologies and social media platforms. These courses can include classes on social media marketing, mobile device usage, or computer skills.
- Photography and Video Production: Many online courses and webinars are available to help retirees improve their photography and video production skills. These courses can include classes on composition, lighting, and editing techniques.
- Art and Design: Online courses and webinars are available to help retirees develop their artistic skills. These courses can include classes on

drawing, painting, sculpture, or graphic design.
- Music Lessons: Online music lessons are available for retirees who want to learn a new instrument or improve their musical skills. These courses can include classes on piano, guitar, singing, or music theory.
- Psychology and Counseling: Online courses and webinars are available to help retirees learn about mental health and wellness. These courses can include topics such as positive psychology, mindfulness, and cognitive-behavioral therapy.
- Business and Entrepreneurship: Online courses and webinars are available to help retirees learn about starting and managing a business. These courses can include topics such as business planning, marketing, and financial management.
- Travel and Culture: Online courses and webinars are available to help retirees learn about travel and culture. These courses can include classes on cultural immersion, world religions, or travel writing.
- Nature and Environmental Studies: Online courses and webinars are available to help retirees learn about nature and the environment. These courses can include classes on wildlife biology, ecology, or environmental conservation.
- STEM Fields: Online courses and webinars are available to help retirees learn about science, technology, engineering, and math (STEM) fields. These courses can include classes on coding, data analysis, or robotics.
- Personal Development: Online courses and webinars are available to help retirees develop new skills and personal interests. These courses can include classes on cooking, gardening, or crafts.

Museum and Art Gallery Visits

Visiting museums and art galleries has long been a popular pastime for people of all ages and backgrounds, and continues to attract millions of visitors every year. For retirees, visiting museums and art galleries can be a great way to learn about history, culture and art, while providing an enjoyable and intellectually stimulating way to spend time.

One of the main benefits of visiting museums and art galleries is the opportunity to view and appreciate a wide range of artworks and artefacts. From ancient civilisations to contemporary art, these institutions offer a wealth of knowledge and inspiration, showcasing the beauty and complexity of human history and culture.

Many museums and galleries also offer guided tours, lectures and workshops to make the learning experience more interactive and engaging. These educational programmes can deepen understanding of the artworks and artefacts on display, providing context and insight into the historical and cultural significance of the exhibits.

Another benefit of visiting museums and galleries is their ability to promote social and community engagement. Many museums and galleries offer events and activities that bring together people with similar interests, providing opportunities to make new friends and connections while learning about art and history.

For retirees, visiting museums and art galleries can also promote cognitive health and mental wellbeing. Studies have shown that engaging in activities that challenge the mind, such as viewing and interpreting art, can help keep the brain sharp and promote healthy ageing.

In addition, visiting museums and art galleries can be a great way for retirees to stay active and engaged in their communities. Many institutions offer senior discounts and special events for retirees, making it more affordable and accessible for them to enjoy cultural experiences and learn about history and art.

Visiting museums and art galleries is a unique and rewarding way for retirees to learn about history, culture and art, while promoting cognitive health and social engagement. With their wide range of exhibitions, guided tours and educational programmes, these institutions are a valuable resource for retirees looking to stay intellectually and socially active in their golden years.

Here are some ideas for museum and art gallery visits that retirees may find interesting and engaging:

- Art Museums: Art museums offer a wealth of opportunities to explore different art movements and styles, from classic to contemporary. Retirees can view paintings, sculptures, and other works of art, and learn more about the artists and their creative processes.
- Science Museums: Science museums provide a fascinating glimpse into the world of science and technology. From exhibits on space exploration to hands-on activities exploring the human body, science museums offer a wide range of experiences that can spark curiosity and promote lifelong learning.
- History Museums: History museums offer a glimpse into the past, allowing retirees to explore different historical periods and events. Whether it involves exhibits on ancient civilizations, colonial history, or world wars, history museums offer a wealth of opportunities to deepen retirees' understanding of the world around them.

- Cultural Museums: Cultural museums offer a glimpse into the traditions, customs, and lifestyles of different cultures around the world. From museums showcasing Native American art and culture to exhibits on African history and traditions, cultural museums provide a fascinating and enriching experience.
- Outdoor Sculpture Parks: Outdoor sculpture parks offer a unique opportunity to experience art in a natural setting. Retirees can explore the beauty and creativity of sculptures and other works of art set against a backdrop of nature.
- Virtual Tours: Many museums and art galleries offer virtual tours, allowing retirees to explore exhibits and collections from the comfort of their own homes. This can be a convenient and flexible way to experience different museums and galleries around the world.
- Photography Exhibits: Photography exhibits offer a glimpse into the world of photography, showcasing a range of techniques and styles. Retirees can view photographs from different eras and photographers, and learn more about the art of photography.
- Architecture Exhibits: Architecture exhibits provide a fascinating look into the world of building design and construction. Retirees can explore the history of architecture and design, and view examples of innovative and influential buildings and structures.
- Botanical Gardens: Botanical gardens offer a peaceful and serene environment for retirees to explore different plants and flowers. Retirees can learn more about the natural world and experience the beauty of different plant species.
- Children's Museums: Children's museums offer a fun and engaging experience for retirees who want to tap into their inner child. Retirees can enjoy hands-on activities, exhibits, and interactive displays that promote learning and exploration.
- Fashion Exhibits: Fashion exhibits offer a glimpse into the world of fashion design and style. Retirees can view clothing and accessories from different eras and designers, and learn more about the evolution of fashion over time.
- Music Museums: Music museums offer a fascinating look into the history of music and different musical genres. Retirees can view exhibits on musicians and composers, and learn more about the cultural and social influences of different musical styles.

Attending Local Science and Technology Fairs

Attending local science and technology fairs is a great way for retirees to stay informed and educated about the latest advances in science and technology. These fairs showcase innovative new technologies, research and developments, providing a hands-on and interactive way to learn about new discoveries and breakthroughs.

One of the main benefits of attending science and technology fairs is the opportunity to explore and experience cutting-edge technology and research in real time. From virtual reality exhibits to robotics demonstrations, these fairs offer a unique opportunity to see the latest advances in science and technology up close and in action.

Many science and technology fairs also offer interactive exhibits and workshops that allow visitors to participate in experiments and demonstrations. This is a fun and engaging way to learn about science and technology, and encourages curiosity and exploration.

Another benefit of attending science and technology fairs is the opportunity to interact with experts in the field. Many fairs feature presentations and talks by scientists and researchers, providing an opportunity to discuss and learn from experts in a variety of fields.

Science and technology fairs also provide opportunities for retirees to stay socially active and involved in their communities. These events often attract large crowds of people with similar interests, giving retirees the chance to make new friends and connections while learning about science and technology.

In addition to promoting curiosity and social engagement, attending science and technology fairs can also promote cognitive health and mental wellbeing. Learning about science and technology challenges the mind and promotes critical thinking, providing a valuable way for retirees to keep their minds sharp and engaged in their golden years.

Attending local science and technology fairs is a great way for retirees to stay informed, educated, and engaged in the latest advancements in science and technology. With their interactive exhibits, expert presentations, and opportunities for social engagement, science and technology fairs provide a fun and rewarding way for retirees to stay intellectually and socially active in their communities.

Here are some ideas for local science and technology fairs that retirees may find interesting and engaging:

• Robotics and Automation: Robotics and automation are rapidly growing fields, and retirees can explore the latest developments and technologies at science and technology fairs. From drones to self-driving cars, robotics and automation are transforming the way we live and work.

- Health and Wellness: Advances in science and technology are revolutionizing the healthcare industry, and retirees can learn more about the latest developments in medical research and technology at science and technology fairs. From new treatments for diseases to wearable health monitoring devices, science and technology are helping to improve our health and wellbeing.
- Green Energy and Sustainability: Green energy and sustainability are becoming increasingly important topics, and retirees can explore the latest developments and technologies in these fields at science and technology fairs. From solar and wind energy to sustainable agriculture and recycling, science and technology are helping to create a more sustainable future.
- Virtual and Augmented Reality: Virtual and augmented reality are transforming the way we experience the world around us, and retirees can explore the latest developments in these technologies at science and technology fairs. From gaming and entertainment to education and training, virtual and augmented reality are changing the way we learn, work, and play.
- Artificial Intelligence: Artificial intelligence is rapidly advancing, and retirees can learn more about the latest developments and applications of AI at science and technology fairs. From autonomous vehicles to smart home devices, AI is changing the way we interact with technology and the world around us.
- Space Exploration: Space exploration is an exciting and inspiring field, and retirees can explore the latest developments and technologies in space exploration at science and technology fairs. From the latest spacecraft and space telescopes to discoveries about our universe, space exploration offers a wealth of opportunities for learning and discovery.
- Artificial limbs and prosthetics: Advances in science and technology have led to significant improvements in the field of artificial limbs and prosthetics. Retirees can learn about the latest advancements in prosthetics, including the use of 3D printing to create customized limbs and the development of robotic prosthetics.
- Nanotechnology: Nanotechnology is the science of manipulating materials at the atomic or molecular level. Retirees can learn about the latest developments in nanotechnology, including the creation of new materials and devices with unique properties.
- Biotechnology: Biotechnology is the use of living organisms or biological systems to create new products or processes. Retirees can explore the latest developments in biotechnology, including genetic engineering, gene therapy, and regenerative medicine.
- Internet of Things (IoT): The Internet of Things (IoT) refers to the network of devices and appliances that are connected to the internet and can communicate with each other. Retirees can learn about the latest developments in IoT, including smart home devices, wearable technology,

and the use of IoT in healthcare and agriculture.

• Cybersecurity: With the increasing reliance on technology in our daily lives, cybersecurity is becoming an increasingly important issue. Retirees can learn about the latest advancements in cybersecurity, including new technologies and strategies for protecting against cyber attacks.

• Renewable Energy: Renewable energy sources like solar and wind power are becoming increasingly important as we seek to reduce our dependence on fossil fuels. Retirees can learn about the latest developments in renewable energy, including new technologies for generating and storing energy, and the use of renewable energy in transportation and agriculture.

Learning a New Language

Learning a new language is a valuable and rewarding pursuit for people of all ages and backgrounds, but it can be particularly beneficial for retirees. Not only does learning a new language provide opportunities for travel and cultural immersion, but it also promotes cognitive health and mental wellbeing.

One of the main benefits of learning a new language is the opportunity to explore new cultures and connect with people from around the world. Retirees who learn a new language can travel to new destinations with greater ease and confidence, engage in meaningful conversations with locals, and gain a deeper understanding and appreciation of different cultures.

As well as increasing cultural awareness, learning a new language can also promote cognitive health and mental wellbeing. Studies have shown that learning a new language challenges the brain and improves memory and cognitive function. In fact, learning a new language has been shown to delay the onset of age-related cognitive decline and Alzheimer's disease.

Another benefit of learning a new language is the opportunity to meet new people and make new friends. Many language learning programmes offer group classes and conversation partners, providing opportunities to connect with people who share similar interests and goals.

Learning a new language can also promote personal growth and development. It requires dedication, patience and perseverance, and can provide a sense of achievement and pride when goals are met. This can be particularly important for retirees who want to continue learning and growing in their golden years.

There are also practical benefits to learning a new language. Retirees who learn a new language may have better career prospects or be able to communicate with non-English speaking family members or carers.

Learning a new language is a valuable and rewarding activity for retirees, offering opportunities for cultural immersion, cognitive health promotion, social engagement, personal growth and practical benefits. With the wide range of language learning programmes and resources available today, it has never been easier for retirees to embark on this enriching and fulfilling journey.

Here are some ideas for learning a new language that retirees may find interesting and engaging:

- Language Classes: Taking formal language classes can be a great way for retirees to learn a new language. Many community colleges and universities offer language courses, and there are also online courses and language learning apps available.
- Language Immersion Programs: Language immersion programs are intensive language-learning experiences that allow retirees to fully immerse themselves in a new language and culture. These programs often involve living with a host family or in a dormitory, and attending language classes and cultural activities.
- Language Exchange Programs: Language exchange programs allow retirees to practice their language skills with native speakers of the language they are learning. This can be a great way to improve fluency and gain a better understanding of the language and culture.
- Language Meetup Groups: Many cities have language meetup groups that allow people to practice their language skills in a casual, social setting. Retirees can meet new people and practice speaking and listening to the language they are learning.
- Language Immersion Travel: Traveling to a country where the language they are learning is spoken can be a great way for retirees to immerse themselves in the language and culture. This can be an exciting and rewarding way to learn a new language while also experiencing a new culture.
- Language Learning Apps: There are many language learning apps available that retirees can use to learn a new language. These apps often include lessons, exercises, and games that make learning a new language fun and engaging.
- Language-based Volunteering: Volunteering with organizations that serve people from the language they are learning can be a great way to practice speaking and listening to the language. This can also be a way to give back to the community while also learning a new language.

• Language Tandem Partners: Retirees can find language tandem partners who are native speakers of the language they are learning and interested in learning their native language. They can practice speaking and listening to the language in a one-on-one setting.

• Language Learning Podcasts: There are many language learning podcasts available that retirees can use to practice listening and speaking to a new language. These podcasts often include conversations, interviews, and news reports in the language they are learning.

• Language Learning Games: There are many language learning games available that can make learning a new language fun and engaging. Games can be a great way to practice vocabulary, grammar, and pronunciation in a playful and relaxed setting.

• Language Learning Books: There are many language learning books available that provide structured lessons and exercises to help retirees learn a new language. Some books also include audio components to help with listening and speaking skills.

• Language Learning Meetups: Many cities have language learning meetups that allow people to practice their language skills in a casual, social setting. Retirees can meet new people and practice speaking and listening to the language they are learning.

Exploring Your Genealogy and Family History

Researching your genealogy and family history is a fascinating and rewarding pursuit that can provide a deep sense of connection to your roots and ancestry. For retirees, delving into family history can be a great way to learn more about their family's origins and heritage, while also promoting personal growth and development.

One of the main benefits of exploring your genealogy and family history is the opportunity to connect with your roots and understand more about your family's origins and history. This can provide a sense of belonging and identity, helping retirees to better understand themselves and their place in the world.

As well as promoting personal growth and development, researching your genealogy and family history can also have practical benefits. Retirees who research their family history can discover valuable information about their health, ancestry and heritage, providing insights that can inform medical decisions, travel plans and more.

Another benefit of exploring your genealogy and family history is the opportunity to connect with family members and distant relatives. Researching family history often involves contacting relatives, sharing stories and memories, and collaborating on research, providing opportunities to connect with family members in a meaningful way.

Exploring your genealogy and family history can also promote cognitive health and mental wellbeing. It requires research, organisation and attention to detail, which challenges the mind and promotes cognitive function. In addition, uncovering new information and insights about family history can provide a sense of accomplishment and pride.

For retirees who are interested in exploring their genealogy and family history, there are a wide range of resources and tools available. Online databases, archives, and genealogy websites provide access to historical records and family trees, while family members and relatives can provide valuable insights and stories.

Exploring your genealogy and family history is a rewarding and enriching pursuit for retirees, providing opportunities for personal growth, connection, and cognitive health promotion. With the wealth of resources and tools available today, retirees have never been in a better position to uncover the fascinating stories and legacies of their family history.

Here are some ideas for exploring your genealogy and family history that retirees may find interesting and engaging:

- Conducting Family Interviews: Retirees can conduct interviews with family members to learn more about their family history. They can ask questions about family traditions, stories, and events that have shaped their family's history.
- Building a Family Tree: Building a family tree can be a great way to visually map out your family's history. There are many online tools and resources available to help retirees build a family tree.
- Visiting Ancestral Homes and Sites: Visiting ancestral homes and sites can be a way to connect with your family history and learn more about your ancestors' lives. Retirees can plan trips to visit the places where their ancestors lived and worked.
- Researching Historical Records: Historical records such as census records, birth and death certificates, and immigration records can provide valuable information about your ancestors. Retirees can use online resources and visit local archives and libraries to access historical records.
- Joining a Genealogy Society: Joining a genealogy society can be a way to connect with others who share an interest in family history. Genealogy societies often provide resources and support for retirees who are interested in exploring their family history.
- Writing a Family History Book: Retirees can write a family history

book to document their family's history and stories. This can be a great way to share family history with future generations.
• Attending Genealogy Conferences: Attending genealogy conferences can be a way to learn new skills and connect with other genealogists. Conferences often offer workshops and lectures on genealogy research and techniques.
• Volunteering at Local Historical Societies: Volunteering at local historical societies can be a way to support and learn about local history. Retirees can work with local historians and archivists to preserve and share historical records.
• Creating a Family History Website: Retirees can create a family history website to share family stories, photos, and genealogy research. This can be a way to connect with family members and share family history with a wider audience.
• Exploring Ethnic and Cultural Heritage: Retirees can explore their ethnic and cultural heritage to learn more about their family's history and traditions. This can involve learning about cultural foods, music, and customs.
• Digitizing Family Records: Digitizing family records such as photographs, letters, and documents can help preserve them for future generations. Retirees can scan and organize these records using online tools and resources.

Attending Lectures and Workshops

Attending lectures and workshops is a valuable way for retirees to continue learning and growing in their golden years. These events provide opportunities to explore new ideas, gain new skills and network with experts in different fields.

One of the main benefits of attending talks and workshops is the opportunity to learn about new topics and ideas. These events cover a wide range of subjects, from history and literature to science and technology, and provide a fun and engaging way to broaden your knowledge and learn new things.

As well as promoting intellectual growth, attending talks and workshops can also provide opportunities for social engagement and networking. These events often attract a diverse crowd of people with similar interests, providing an opportunity to make new friends and connections while engaging in meaningful conversation.

Attending talks and workshops can also promote personal growth and development. Learning new skills or gaining new knowledge can provide a sense of achievement and pride, helping retirees to feel fulfilled and engaged in their daily lives.

Another benefit of attending talks and workshops is the opportunity to network with experts in different fields. Many events feature presentations and talks by industry leaders and experts, providing an opportunity to engage in discussions and learn from experienced professionals.

As well as attending face-to-face lectures and workshops, retirees can also participate in online events and webinars. These provide a convenient and accessible way to engage in lifelong learning from the comfort of your own home.

Attending lectures and workshops is a valuable way for retirees to continue learning and growing in their golden years. With opportunities for intellectual growth, social engagement, personal development and expert insight, these events are a fun and rewarding way for retirees to stay intellectually and socially active in their communities.

Here are some ideas for attending lectures and workshops that retirees may find interesting and engaging:

• Lifelong Learning Programs: Many universities and community centers offer lifelong learning programs that allow retirees to attend lectures and workshops on a variety of topics. These programs often offer classes in the arts, humanities, and sciences.
• Industry Conferences: Retirees can attend industry conferences to learn about new developments in their field of interest. This can be a way to stay up-to-date with the latest trends and connect with others in their field.
• Cultural Events: Cultural events such as museum exhibits, art shows, and theater performances often include lectures and workshops that provide a deeper understanding of the art or culture being presented.
• Personal Development Workshops: Personal development workshops can help retirees explore new interests and develop new skills. These workshops can include classes in writing, meditation, or creative arts.
• Professional Development Workshops: Professional development workshops can help retirees develop new skills or refresh their knowledge in a particular field. These workshops can include classes in marketing, finance, or leadership.
• Book Clubs: Book clubs provide a way for retirees to engage in intellectual discussions with others who share their interests. Retirees can join local book clubs or online book clubs to discuss literature and ideas.
• Guest Speaker Series: Many libraries, museums, and community centers host guest speaker series that cover a wide range of topics.

Retirees can attend these events to hear from experts in fields such as science, history, and the arts.

• Technology Workshops: Technology workshops can help retirees learn new digital skills such as coding, social media marketing, or website design. These skills can be useful for starting a new hobby or business venture in retirement.

• Environmental Conservation Workshops: Retirees can attend environmental conservation workshops to learn about sustainability and how to live a more eco-friendly lifestyle. These workshops can include classes in composting, renewable energy, or gardening.

• Creative Writing Workshops: Creative writing workshops can help retirees explore their creative side and express themselves through writing. These workshops can include classes in memoir writing, fiction writing, or poetry.

• Cooking Workshops: Cooking workshops can help retirees learn new culinary skills and techniques. These workshops can include classes in regional cuisines, healthy cooking, or baking.

• Travel Workshops: Travel workshops can help retirees plan and prepare for their next adventure. These workshops can include classes in budget travel, cultural immersion, or adventure travel.

CONCLUSION

Retirement marks the beginning of a new chapter in your life, filled with endless possibilities and opportunities for personal growth, fulfilment and happiness. While it can be a time of change and transition, it is also an opportunity to reflect on your values, interests and goals, and to make conscious choices that align with your vision of a fulfilling retirement.

Creating a fulfilling and purposeful retirement means taking time to explore new hobbies, learn new skills and try new experiences. It also means staying engaged with loved ones, friends and communities, and giving back through volunteering or philanthropy. By embracing change and new opportunities, retirees can make the most of their retirement years and create a life that is rich, meaningful and rewarding.

At the heart of a fulfilling retirement is a sense of purpose and passion. Whether it is pursuing a lifelong dream, exploring a new interest or spending more time with loved ones, retirees can find joy and fulfilment in the things that matter most to them. By staying connected to their values and interests, retirees can cultivate a sense of purpose and meaning that will carry them through their golden years.

Another key element of a fulfilling retirement is embracing new technologies and opportunities for lifelong learning. With the advent of digital technologies, retirees have more access than ever to online courses, webinars and other educational resources that can promote intellectual growth and cognitive health. Whether it is learning a new language, researching family history, or attending lectures and workshops, retirees can stay intellectually engaged and socially active by embracing these new technologies and opportunities.

Retirement offers a unique opportunity to create a life that is fulfilling, purposeful, and rewarding. By embracing change, staying engaged with loved ones and communities, and exploring new hobbies and interests, retirees can make the most of this exciting new chapter in their lives. With the right mindset and a sense of purpose and passion, retirement can be a time of growth, connection, and joy.

Creating a Fulfilling and Purposeful Retirement

Creating a fulfilling and purposeful retirement is a process that involves reflection, intentionality and a commitment to personal growth and development. It starts with taking the time to reflect on your values, interests and goals, and identifying the things that bring you joy and fulfilment. By understanding your priorities and passions, you can create a roadmap for your retirement that aligns with your vision of a meaningful and rewarding life.

An important aspect of creating a fulfilling and purposeful retirement is staying engaged with your community and loved ones. Retirement offers a unique opportunity to invest in meaningful relationships and cultivate deeper connections with the people who matter most to you. Whether it is spending more time with family, joining a social club or volunteering in your community, staying connected to others can provide a sense of belonging and purpose that is essential to a fulfilling retirement.

Another key element of a fulfilling retirement is exploring new hobbies, interests and experiences. Retirement is an opportunity to try new things and pursue lifelong dreams that may have been put on hold during your working years. Whether it is travelling to new destinations, learning a new language or exploring a new hobby, pursuing your passions can provide a sense of fulfilment and purpose that can enhance your retirement experience.

Creating a fulfilling and purposeful retirement also involves a commitment to personal growth and development. Retirement offers opportunities for lifelong learning and intellectual growth, whether through online courses, workshops or other educational resources. By challenging yourself to learn new skills and gain new knowledge, you can stay mentally sharp and engaged, promoting cognitive health and well-being.

At the heart of a fulfilling retirement is a sense of purpose and meaning. By staying connected with your values and passions, and investing in meaningful relationships and experiences, you can create a retirement that is rich, rewarding, and fulfilling. Whether it involves pursuing a lifelong dream or simply spending more time with loved ones, creating a fulfilling and purposeful retirement is about embracing the things that bring you joy and fulfillment, and living life to the fullest.

Embracing Change and New Opportunities

Embracing change and new opportunities is an important aspect of a fulfilling retirement. Retirement marks a significant transition in life, and it is natural to feel uncertain or anxious about the changes it brings. However, by embracing change and new opportunities, retirees can create a retirement that is rich, rewarding and fulfilling.

One of the most important benefits of embracing change and new opportunities is personal growth and development. Retirement provides an opportunity to try new things and stretch yourself outside your comfort zone, which promotes personal growth and development. Whether it is exploring a new hobby or learning a new skill, trying new things can help retirees stay engaged and intellectually stimulated, promoting cognitive health and well-being.

Embracing change and new opportunities can also promote social engagement and connectedness. Retirement can be a time when social networks shift or change, and it is important to stay connected to others to maintain a sense of belonging and purpose. By trying new experiences and engaging with new people, retirees can expand their social circles and make new connections that promote social and emotional wellbeing.

Another benefit of embracing change and new opportunities is the chance to pursue passions and interests that may have been put on hold during working years. Retirement offers the opportunity to explore new hobbies, travel to new destinations and pursue lifelong dreams that may have been put on hold during working years. By pursuing passions and interests, retirees can create a fulfilling and rewarding retirement that promotes a sense of purpose and meaning in life.

Finally, embracing change and new opportunities can promote adaptability and resilience. Retirement is a time of change and transition, and by embracing new experiences, retirees can develop the skills and mindset to adapt to new challenges and situations. By cultivating a spirit of adaptability and resilience, retirees can navigate the ups and downs of retirement with grace and resilience, promoting mental and emotional wellbeing.

Embracing change and new opportunities is an important aspect of a fulfilling retirement. By encouraging personal growth and development, social engagement and connection, pursuing passions and interests, and cultivating adaptability and resilience, retirees can create a retirement that is rich, rewarding and fulfilling. With an open mind and a willingness to embrace new experiences, retirees can make the most of their golden years and create a life that is truly fulfilling and purposeful.

REVIEW THIS BOOK

Dear Reader,

I am truly grateful for your time and attention in reading my book. It would mean the world to me if you could take a moment to leave a review on Amazon and share your thoughts on my work. I value your honest feedback, so if there are any areas where you feel that I can improve, please do let me know.

If you enjoyed reading my book and found it to be informative and inspiring, I would like to extend my heartfelt appreciation to you. Your positive review would mean a lot to me and would motivate me to continue dedicating my time and energy to creating more valuable content.

Thank you for your support and encouragement, and I wish you all the best on your own personal journey. Keep up the amazing work!

Wishing you the best.